D1034807

PEACE AMONG CHRISTIANS

PEACE AMONG CHRISTIANS

Augustin Cardinal Bea
and
Willem A. Visser 't Hooft

Translated by Judith Moses

ASSOCIATION PRESS
HERDER AND HERDER

1967
HERDER AND HERDER NEW YORK
232 Madison Avenue, New York 10016

ASSOCIATION PRESS
291 Broadway, New York 10007

Nihil obstat: Brendan W. Lawlor, Censor Librorum
Imprimatur: ✠ Robert F. Joyce, Bishop of Burlington
May 15, 1967

Contents

Introduction

BY BISHOP J. G. M. WILLEBRANDS

FOR THE FIRST time, the "German Book Trade Peace Prize" was awarded to two persons simultaneously: to His Eminence Augustin Cardinal Bea, President of the Secretariat for Promoting Christian Unity, in Rome, and to Dr. Willem Adolf Visser 't Hooft, Secretary General of the World Council of Churches, in Geneva.

Cardinal Bea and Dr. Visser 't Hooft do, indeed, have common bonds. Both are not only working to achieve peace and unity among Christians; their common interests are an actual symbol of this peace. Peace may exist between two persons, and among many people. It signifies a personal relationship either between individuals or between communities. Any type of peace is based, in principle, on an "I-thou" relationship deriving from the union of God and man in Christ. In the Scriptures, peace in Christ is described as a bond which unites all who believe in Him; ". . . maintain the unity of the Spirit in the bond of peace" (Eph. 4, 3).

This peace is dynamic, creative. Matthias Laros gave the following title to his book on the unity of Christians: *Creative Peace*. Peace comes from God through Christ; it is the spirit of Christ. Spirit is the principle of unity in the community of those who believe in Christ and in the Church of Christ.

The unity of the Church was described as follows in the Acts of the Apostles (9, 31): "So the church throughout all Judea and Galilee and Samaria had peace and was built up; and walking in the fear of the Lord and in the comfort of the Holy Spirit it was multiplied."

The ecumenical movement is directed towards reëstablishing this peace among the Churches, and towards leading them back to a unity of the Spirit through the bond of peace.

This movement assumed an official, world-wide character when nearly all Christian Churches and congregations outside of the Catholic Church joined the World Council of Churches, which is a community of Churches: "The World Council of Churches is a community of Churches who, in accordance with the Holy Scriptures, acknowledge Jesus Christ as God and Saviour, and who therefore endeavor to carry out this view by means of joint effort, for which purpose they are called upon for the glory of God, the Father, the Son, and the Holy Spirit" (New Delhi, 1961).

The ecumenical movement assumed its official form in the Catholic Church through the efforts of Pope John XXIII, when he convoked a Council which "will not only aim towards a strengthening of Christian peoples, but which also will serve as an invitation to the separated communities to regain the unity longed for today by so many hearts in all places throughout the earth" (*L'Osservatore Romano,* January 26/27, 1959).

In his opening address to the second session of the Council, Pope Paul VI affirmed this reëstablishment of Christian unity as being the main purpose of the Council. The Council itself, in its *Decree on Ecumenism,* recognized and described the ecumenical movement from the point of view of Catholicism's basic principles.

This book is dedicated to two persons who played a leading

role in the ecumenical movement: Cardinal Bea and Dr. Visser 't Hooft. Since the founding of the Secretariat for Promoting Christian Unity, they have kept in touch with each other not only out of mutual personal respect, but also for the sake of their common concern with common responsibility towards Jesus Christ. Through their concerted effort they were able to continue their work, preceding from the basis already established by means of personal contacts between Catholic theologians and theologians of the World Council and also, since 1952, between the Catholic Conference on Ecumenical Problems and the staff of the World Council. (Many of these contacts were established during and after the Second World War.)

How did this personal association between Cardinal Bea and Dr. Visser 't Hooft come about? In order to answer this question correctly it is both necessary and interesting to turn back to the founding of the Secretariat for Promoting Christian Unity.

In May of 1960 Dr. Frans Thijssen and the author of this introduction were in Italy. Starting in February of every year, a discussion between Catholics and Waldensians took place in Milan, so we attended a meeting held at the apartment of Minister Ribet in Milan. In order to know the Waldensians better, we visited Torre Pellice. We held a conference in Pinerolo, where eight ministers from the Waldensian Church and several laymen were present.

It was our job to prepare a meeting of the Catholic Conference on Ecumenical Problems. It was to be held in Gazzada (Northern Italy) in September of 1960. For this purpose we also visited His Eminence Cardinal Montini in Milan. It just so happened that the Cardinal had arranged a "Piccolo Sinodo" (little synod) of the deans of the diocese on the same days for which the Gazzada Conference had been planned. Despite this fact he wanted to try to come to Gazzada one afternoon.

Another reason for our trip was the question whether or not Catholic observers at the Faith and Order Conference held in St. Andrews, Scotland, August 3–15, 1960, should also be sent to the subsequent meeting of the Central Committee of the World Council of Churches held from August 16 to 24, 1960, also in St. Andrews, and finally, to the Plenary Meeting of the World Council in New Delhi (1961). Dr. Visser 't Hooft had asked me to deal with these questions in Rome, and had written to me to this effect.

For this purpose we visited the Holy Office in Rome as well as His Eminence Cardinal Bea, with whom we had been in the habit of discussing our ecumenical problems for years.

The Cardinal informed us that the Pope was soon to issue a *Motu proprio* in which an announcement of the founding of a Secretariat for Promoting Christian Unity would be made. By means of this Secretariat the Church expressed its desire to take an official active part in ecumenical problems.

The Pope personally informed Cardinal Bea that he had been selected to head the Secretariat. A Secretariat, not a commission, was founded to deal with ecumenical issues, thereby allowing the possibility for freer structure and method of work.

It was clear that this was of greatest importance for the ecumenical movement. How often had the complaint been made, and in particular to Dr. Visser 't Hooft, that there was no office in the Catholic Church to which one could turn concerning ecumenical problems. That had become very clear as a result of the misunderstandings which occurred at the meeting of the

Central Committee of the World Council which took place in Rhodes in 1959.

However, prior to the issuance of the *Motu proprio,* we had to return to Holland. On our way back we were able to pass through Geneva. Cardinal Bea expressly instructed me to go to Geneva and explain the founding of the Secretariat to Dr. Visser 't Hooft in his behalf. Furthermore, Cardinal Bea himself wanted to meet Dr. Visser 't Hooft unofficially. "I cannot invite him to Rome, and I cannot go to Geneva myself," he said.

The meeting was supposed to take place somewhere on neutral territory. The Cardinal intended to go to Munich for the Eucharistic Congress, and then remain in Freiburg im Breisgau from August 12 to August 15. He also wanted to visit the meeting of the Catholic Conference on Ecumenical Problems in Gazzada (September 19–24). He would be in Milan for this occasion. "Tell Dr. Visser 't Hooft that I would do this with the greatest of pleasure and joy. Dr. Visser 't Hooft should tell me himself whether and how he considers such a meeting possible."

On June 8 Dr. Frans Thijssen and I visited Dr. Visser 't Hooft to inform him, in behalf of Cardinal Bea, of the founding of the Secretariat. The exact name was not yet known at the time. (Pope John himself was to call it the *"Secretariatus ad christianorum unitatem fovendam"* only at a later date.)

Dr. Visser 't Hooft was extremely pleased about the news. From that point on, the World Council would be able to turn to this Secretariat in its contacts with the Catholic Church.

He was delighted to accept the proposal for an unofficial meeting with Cardinal Bea to discuss the new situation and its consequences. September 22 was suggested as the date, and

11

Milan was selected as the place for the meeting. In addition, I brought him the reply from Rome concerning the observers who were supposed to attend the Faith and Order Conference and the Central Committee meeting in St. Andrews. Dr. Visser 't Hooft expressed his particular joy at Cardinal Bea having been appointed president of the new Secretariat. Dr. H. H. Harms had always spoken very enthusiastically about Cardinal Bea upon returning from his trips to Rome.

The Central Committee held its meetings in St. Andrews from August 16 to 24, 1960. The new developments within the Catholic Church and the relationship of the World Council to the Catholic Church were discussed in detail both in the Executive Committee's report and in the Secretary General's report.

The Executive Committee stated its view on the following five points:

(1) The fact that a dialogue with the Roman Catholic Church will be possible is warmly received.

(2) However, it is to be hoped that, due to this new development, the informal talks held to date between Roman Catholic theologians and theologians of other Churches will not be completely suppressed in the future by talks of a more official nature, because for the present time this very sort of informal talk can best serve the purpose of eliminating misunderstandings.

(3) No Church should be afraid that the World Council will attempt to speak for or act in behalf of its member Churches in questions concerning Church unity. According to its charter, the World Council is not authorized to act in behalf of its member Churches in such matters. Each Church makes its own decisions in this area with complete freedom.

12

This, of course, is a prerequisite for us. However, we must mention the fact that the question arises from time to time as to whether the World Council intends to hold informal or formal discussions with the Roman Catholic Church in matters of Church unity. The answer is that in view of the nature of our movement, this should not be a consideration in any case.

(4) However, the World Council may use any opportunities which might offer themselves to inform the new Secretariat of certain basic views which the Plenary Meeting or Central Committee might advocate (such as, for example, those concerning freedom of belief or in the area of social problems).

(5) It should be borne in mind that formation of the Secretariat does not mean that any of the basic differences existing between the Roman Catholic Church and the Churches within the World Council will be shelved. On the contrary, this act signifies a change in procedure and atmosphere. The point in question is to seize the opportunity for discussion, and this means that the real problems will be placed in the foreground. Our job, in this dialogue, will be to explain the knowledge God allowed us to acquire together during the fifty years subsequent to the founding of our movement.

The meeting between Cardinal Bea and Dr. Visser 't Hooft took place in the Centro San Fedele in Milan on September 22, 1960. This was an historical moment even though the meeting did have an unofficial nature and knowledge of it was not passed on to the press.

Cardinal Bea expressed his satisfaction with the five points set forth by the Executive Committee, and which he was pleased to pass on then to the Pope. Dr. Visser 't Hooft affirmed the positive direction being headed towards not only by the founding of the Secretariat, but also by the personality of its president. Both the president and the secretary of the Secretariat had been on good terms with the World Council for quite some time. Further discussion was held concerning the possibility of sending Catholic observers to the New Delhi Assembly, the continuation of unofficial contacts between the Catholic Church and the World Council of Churches by means of the "Catholic Conference on Ecumenical Problems" (see Report of the Executive Committee *b*), and also concerning modernization within the Church and religious freedom.

It was also discussed how Christians of other Churches might take part in the Council, and, in particular, whether Council observers might be permitted. The Secretariat was supposed to draft a set of rules governing the task and position of these observers.

Dr. Visser 't Hooft assured us that the World Council of Churches would not be able to speak in behalf of the other Churches in this regard. However, he could advise us as to the method and means by which we might establish contact with these other Churches. On this occasion an unofficial meeting on "Religious Freedom as a Problem Among Churches" was arranged between representatives of the World Council of Churches and Catholic theologians from the Conference on Ecumenical Problems. This discussion was planned to be held during the second half of March 1961. The New Delhi Assembly would most certainly also deal with the problem of religious freedom, and it could be assumed that the Vatican Council would also speak about it.

The first Plenary Assembly of the Secretariat for Promoting Christian Unity took place in Rome on November 14 and 15,

1960. Sub-committees were formed to carry out the work the Secretariat had in mind. One of the jobs of these sub-committees was to study the ecumenical movement under way among those of our brethren with whom connections had been severed, and, in particular, to study the World Council. This study represented the first preparatory effort towards the drafting of the decree on the ecumenical movement.

A second meeting between Cardinal Bea and Dr. Visser 't Hooft, one just as unofficial as the first, took place in Rome (December 3, 1960) at the Secretariat for Promoting Christian Unity. It took place immediately following the departure of the Archbishop of Canterbury, Dr. Fisher, but had nothing to do with the visit of the Anglican Primate. A delegation from the World Council of Churches was on its way to South Africa (Dr. Franklin Clark Fry, Dr. Visser 't Hooft, and Dr. Niesel), had some time between flights, and used this time to pay a brief visit. The contacts which already existed were renewed, and the possibility of Catholic observers in New Delhi was discussed in more concrete terms.

These first meetings were of utmost importance because they proved that from the very beginning Cardinal Bea was aware of the deep meaning the World Council of Churches had within the ecumenical movement. Here he found a goal-conscious and organized movement for the unity of almost all Christian Churches. Dr. Visser 't Hooft, for his part, saw and accepted the significance of the Secretariat as an official address with which to establish contact with the Catholic Church, and he bestowed his complete trust on the person who was the president of this Secretariat.

In compliance with the wishes of the Central Committee in

15

St. Andrews, unofficial contacts between the World Council and Catholic theologians were continued even after the founding of the Secretariat for Promoting Christian Unity. These contacts had proven very useful since the emergence of the ecumenical movement.

The Catholic Conference on Ecumenical Problems and the World Council jointly organized two important conferences for the following year on the subject of religious freedom (May 1–12, 1961) and on the World Faith and Order Conference in Montreal (March 18–23, 1963).

The most significant event which occurred in the 1961 ecumenical movement was the Third Plenary Assembly of the World Council of Churches (November 19 to December 6, 1961). On this occasion the Catholic Church, for the first time, sent official observers, thus involving the Secretariat in the movement. This delegation was of prime importance to the Secretariat. It represented an expression of the spirit of brotherhood among Christians, just as Pope John had wanted and succeeded in creating on numerous occasions. It was a means of exchanging information, and, even beyond this, a means of acquiring direct knowledge about each other's intentions. It was a step leading to a dialogue between the Catholic Church and the Churches participating in the World Council of Churches.

The Plenary Assembly expressed its joy at this development on several different occasions. In the report drawn up by the Guidance Committee on Questions of Principle, the following was stated concerning relationships towards non-member Churches: "[The Assembly] welcomes the closer contacts which have evolved in recent times with certain Roman Catholic theologians and other Roman Catholic churchmen who hold Christian unity dear to their hearts. It also hopes that these contacts will become progressively more fruitful in the future. The Plenary Assembly hereby wishes to express its joy at the fact that a number of churches, including the Roman Catholic Church, are present. It wishes to place in the heart and conscience of member churches the importance of unending prayer for their Christian brethren throughout the world" (New Delhi, 1961, Documentary Report on the Third Plenary Assembly of the Ecumenical Council of Churches, p. 169).

In his report entitled "Mache den Raum deines Zeltes weit," Dr. Visser 't Hooft said:

"In this connection we must also talk about new developments regarding the Roman Catholic Church. Since the beginning of the World Council, there have been contacts with individual Roman Catholics who have been very interested in the ecumenical movement, and who have often indicated such in their publications, many of which were of great value and posed problems well worth considering. Today, in addition to these contacts, we have unofficial though very useful association with the special Secretariat created for us by Pope John XXIII for the purpose of promoting unity among Christians. Therefore, we are pleased at this time to greet as observers to our Plenary Assembly five Roman Catholics who have been selected and authorized by the Secretariat. The nature of our association with the Secretariat is based upon mutual exchange of information pertaining to subjects of mutual concern. In this way we were able to bring up several special issues, such as, for example, the question of religious freedom, which we were pleased to see could be clarified by the approaching Second

Vatican Council. Looking at the Council itself, we share Professor Schlink's conviction about connections between the New Delhi Plenary Assembly and the Vatican Council, which he described as follows: 'It would undoubtedly mean a great deal to Christianity and to the world if it would become apparent, on the basis of decisions reached by each side, that these two Councils were not convening against one another, and that each of them did not seek to discover itself therein, but rather sought only to serve Jesus Christ'" (Chapter 1, pp. 530–531).

In the apostolic constitution *Humane Salutis* of December 25, 1961, Pope John officially convoked the 1962 Vatican Council. In this document, the Pope addressed all Christians not associated with the See of St. Peter with the following words:

"To this chorus of prayers, we invite also all Christians of Churches separated from Rome, that the Council may be also to their advantage. We know that many of these sons are anxious for a return of unity and of peace, according to the teachings and the prayer of Christ to the Father. And we know also that the announcement of the Council has been accepted by them not only with joy but also that not a few have already promised to offer their prayers for its success, and that they hope to send representatives of their communities to follow its work at close quarters. All this is for us a reason of great comfort and of hope, and precisely for the purpose of facilitating these contacts we instituted the Secretariat some time ago for this specific purpose."

In the meantime, the Secretariat drew up a statute for Council observers. It was approved by the Pope and accepted by the "Ordo Concilii Vaticani celebrandi."

On April 3, 1962, a meeting between the president and the

secretary general of the World Council of Churches took place in the World Council administration building, route de Malagnou, Geneva. Dr. Visser 't Hooft made arrangements for the Secretary of the Secretariat to have the opportunity to report there on the possibility, position, and function of Council observers from other Christian Churches. A very useful discussion concerning the manner of issuing invitations followed thereupon. The following sects were represented: the Lutheran World Federation, the World Presbyterian Alliance, the World Methodist Council, the Baptist World Alliance, the International Congregational Council, the World Convention of the Churches of Christ (Disciples), the Friends World Committee for Consultation. Also present were: staff members of the World Council of Churches, the representative of the Constantinople Patriarchate at the World Council, the representative of the Moscow Patriarchate at the World Council, a representative of the high-Catholic Churches and a representative of the Whitsun congregations. A discussion was also held with Dr. Visser 't Hooft, acting as secretary general of the World Council.

These discussions were of tremendous importance to further contacts between the Council and the Reform Churches. Everything which followed took place in an atmosphere of frankness and trust.

At the meeting of the Central Committee in Paris (August 7–16, 1962) the World Council of Churches decided to accept the invitation to send observers to the Council.

"It was decided,

"that the Central Committee accepts the invitation extended by the Vatican Secretariat to send one or two observers to the

Second Vatican Council for the purpose of promoting Christian unity.

"It is clear,

"that the purpose of sending these observers is to obtain direct information about the work of the Vatican Council, which will consider a variety of issues pertaining to relations between Churches and to Christian unity in general;

"that the observers may not be authorized to speak officially in behalf of the World Council of Churches or its member Churches, and that they may not take part in any negotiations whatsoever in its behalf; however, they shall be able to offer informal explanations of the attitudes of the World Council of Churches as these have been set forth in decisions taken at meetings or by the Central Committee;

"that the observers may be given advice by authorized persons from the World Council of Churches during the Council meeting" (Minutes and Reports of the Sixteenth Meeting of the Central Committee of the WCC. Paris, France, August 7–16, 1962).

In his report to the Central Committee, Dr. Visser 't Hooft, in his address entitled "In the Year of the Second Vatican Council," spoke about what this Council meant to a major part of Christianity. The World Council must have had the feeling that this was indeed its very own problem. It was something new for Catholic observers to attend a meeting of the World Council of Churches and for observers from the World Council to be invited to a Council held by the Roman Catholic Church. This new attitude, based upon dialogue, had to have certain consequences. (The complete text of the report rendered by the Secretary General may be found in this book, pp. 70–73.)

This decision marked the beginning of a new development in relations between the World Council and the Secretariat. (I am, of course, limiting myself, in this Introduction, to specific dealings between these two bodies.) These relations were consolidated by the presence of observers in Rome and by direct contacts between the two staffs. On January 8, 1963, while travelling to Nairobi for the All-African Youth Conference, Dr. Visser 't Hooft paid a visit to Cardinal Bea in Rome. The spirit of the meeting was also expressed in the telegram sent by the World Council to Cardinal Bea upon the death of Pope John. Dr. Lukas Vischer represented the World Council at the funeral ceremony.

In the meanwhile, the Secretariat, together with the Commission for the Eastern Churches and the Theological Commission, worked out a plan for the ecumenical movement. It was sent to the Council Fathers in May 1963 and put up for discussion on November 18, 1963.

The Catholic Conference on Ecumenical Problems met in Gazzada (Northern Italy) from August 26–31, 1963, to deal with the theme: "La situation œcuménique à l'heure du Concile." The secretary of the Conference posed the following question in his opening speech:

"Is a study pertaining to dialogue possible? A dialogue presupposes certain conditions. Are these conditions present in the Secretariat, in the Council? This study was possible because the dialogue which took place during the preceding years had been well prepared. It had been prepared by ecumenical centers, theologians, and first-class ecumenical workers. It had been a point of concern in magazines, at congresses, conferences, and student meetings. It had been favored by the prayer of the

21

people of God. History can give due credit to the following few names: Cardinal Mercier, Dom Lambert Beauduin, Pope John XXIII, Father Paul Wattson, Father Couturier, Cathedral Provost Paul Simon, Father Max Pribilla. One could easily add to this list of names. I am omitting the names of those who are still carrying on this work. I would also like to call to mind the names of those who have since passed away, for they are still present in spirit in the Secretariat's work."

Dr. Lukas Vischer, who attended the first session of the Vatican Council meeting as an observer, delivered a full report on it to the World Council. At a meeting in Rochester, New York (August 26 to September 2, 1963), he spoke about the Vatican Council as a support for the World Council, both in its Executive Committee and, finally, in its Central Committee.

On the occasion of this Central Committee meeting, Dr. Visser 't Hooft, in reference to the Catholic Church, stated that one of the most important ecumenical steps to be accomplished was when the majority of the Catholic bishops expressed their distinct desire to play a positive and active role in ecumenical problems. He then described the hard truths which remained and the specific temptations and dangers which the establishment of various centers born of ecumenical initiative might imply. He also defined the line of action which might be taken for the future. (For the text of this report, see pp. 76–89.)

It became clear, as early as during the first session of the Vatican Council, that a conversation between the Catholic Church and the other Christian Churches and communities was a possibility for the future, and even on an official level. This was due in greatest measure to Pope John. The orientation and leadership he offered the Council, the spirit of brotherhood with which he addressed the observers from other Churches as he welcomed them, all this was indicative of the difference in Catholic attitude towards Christians divided among themselves as compared to the attitude of the Council of Trent or the First Vatican Council.

The World Council of Churches gave the new situation due consideration. The desire arose in the Secretariat for Promoting Christian Unity as well as in the World Council for an oriented discussion of future possibilities based upon an analysis of the new ecumenical situation.

This discussion took place in Milan on April 15, 1964. It had a confidential nature. The goal on both sides was to acquire clear insight into the problems and possibilities of future relations between both bodies. At this meeting Cardinal Bea and Dr. Visser 't Hooft met once again. And once again Dr. Lukas Vischer, Dr. Nikos Nissiotis, Msgr. Johannes Willebrands, Father Jérôme Hamer, O.P., and Father Pierre Duprey took part in the discussion.

These talks could be no more than preliminary and instructive in nature. It was decided that the staffs would remain in contact with each other. A mixed study group to examine the principles and concrete means of collaborated efforts was envisaged. Questions pertaining to faith and Church order were also dealt with, as were those pertaining to practical matters which cause difficulties in Church life. Everyone agreed that nothing could be done prior to issuance of the decree on the ecumenical movement, because this decree would first have to define the Catholic principles of practice. However, it was hoped that the study group would soon be able to begin its work.

Subsequent to the Milan meeting, the study was begun, and each side took more careful stock of itself. During the third Council meeting the *Decree on Ecumenism* underwent its final editing. It was promulgated on November 21, 1964.

The World Council of Churches, at the July, 1964, meeting of its Executive Committee in Tutzing, dealt with the relationship of the World Council to the Catholic Church.

This study concerned ecclesiology, above all. The following questions were brought up in this connection: the unity and harmony of the Church and the fact that several Churches exist; the difference between the Catholic Church, on the one hand, with its sense of ecclesiastical duty and sense of responsibility as a Church, and, on the other hand, the World Council, which is a council of Churches; the necessity, on the one hand, for direct links between the Catholic Church and other individual Churches and Church communities, and, on the other hand, for the inviolable interrelationship of all of these common bonds within the framework of the ecumenical movement as a whole; the meeting of the two Churches as equals, and their mutually coordinated efforts in the ecumenical movement; the significance of the World Council as an organ and expression of Church fellowship within the ecumenical movement. Concrete possibilities for collaboration were sought.

These preparatory contacts resulted in a detailed statement made by the Central Committee of the World Council in Enugu, January 12–21, 1965 (see minutes and reports of the Eighteenth Meeting, pp. 36–39).

The most important point made in this statement was the suggestion "that a study group be set up composed of eight representatives from the World Council of Churches and six representatives from the Roman Catholic Church. The job of this group would be to work out the principles to be observed for future collaboration and the methods to be used in doing so. In its discussion of special areas of study, the group could invite personalities who specialize in these areas to take part as consultants. The purpose of the study group is not to arrive at decisions, whatever their nature might be, but to work out proposals to be submitted to the respective Church bodies they represent, which this body should then pass on to its member Churches" (Chapter 1, p. 38).

The difficulties which resulted at the end of the third conference period of the Vatican Council with regard to ecumenical attitudes and problems were discussed realistically yet in a fraternal manner by Dr. Visser 't Hooft when he was in Enegu. In his report to the Central Committee he spoke about relations with the Catholic Church and the difficulties these imply. (For the text of this report, see pp. 89-99.)

But difficulties do not delay the progress made in the World Council. Participation of the Catholic Church will automatically imply various new difficulties. However, more to be feared would be aloofness or even exclusion by others, which would bring the ecumenical movement to a standstill.

These difficulties will have to be overcome by the sort of faith that moves mountains. The Council was well aware of these difficulties when it concluded its *Decree on Ecumenism* with the following words:

"This most sacred Synod . . . declares its realization that the holy task of reconciling all Christians in the unity of the one and only Church of Christ transcends human energies and abilities. It therefore places its hope entirely in the prayer of

Christ for the Church, in the love of the Father for us, and in the power of the Holy Spirit. 'And hope does not disappoint us, because God's love has been poured into our hearts through the Holy Spirit which has been given to us' (Rom. 5, 5)."

This is the spirit in which Christians in the World Council work together. The trust they render one another is based on the spirit of Christ, the spirit upon which the principle of unity within the Church is based.

On February 18, 1965, Cardinal Bea paid an official visit to the World Council in Geneva. Visiting there at the same time was Pastor Marc Boegner, one of the founders and first European presidents of the World Council. The reception was both festive and filled with the spirit of brotherhood. Everyone felt that this was an historic moment. The Cardinal's visit assumed a very special meaning because he delivered the Catholic Church's official answer to the proposal made by the Central Committee in Enugu:

"I am especially happy to state on this occasion, that the Holy See welcomes with joy and accepts fully and completely the proposal made by the Central Committee of the Ecumenical Council in Enugu last year to the effect that a mixed committee be set up composed of eight representatives from the World Council and six representatives from the Catholic Church whose goal it will be to explore together the possibilities for dialogue and cooperation between the Council and the Catholic Church" (Rencontre Oecuménique à Genève, Geneva 1965, pp. 32–33).

A new period in relations between the Catholic Church and the World Council of Churches was entered into. The evolution which the Council was at the point of setting into motion had become manifest on the basis of concrete fact. Dr. Visser 't Hooft confirmed this in his reply:

"The fact that your Church and the World Council of Churches have now publically expressed their wish to develop interrelations is indeed an historic one. Now work may begin."

I shall conclude this Introduction herewith. Cardinal Bea and Dr. Visser 't Hooft, each by himself and both together, have played an important and responsible part in this development. They have done so in order to serve the Church of Christ and obey the call and mercy of God. May the Prince of Peace bless their efforts!

Introduction

BY EUGENE CARSON BLAKE

THAT the ecumenical movement continues to move is perhaps the most obvious conclusion that one must draw from reading this book. On the Roman Catholic side, both from the historical introduction of Bishop Willebrands and the several addresses and press conference reports by Cardinal Bea, there is revealed the fascinating story of the official entrance of the largest Christian Church into the "loyal dialogue" which has been from the beginning the style and ethos of the ecumenical movement. On the other hand, the reports to the Central Committee of the World Council of Churches by its former General Secretary, Dr. Visser 't Hooft, and the selection of his addresses contained in this book, are a remarkably unified story of the effect upon the Council of the renewal and new stance of the Roman Catholic Church set, however, in the wider historical perspective of what God has been doing in the past sixty years among all the Christian Churches.

It is fortunate that, since the World Council of Churches and the Roman Catholic Church are not comparable entities (one is a council of Churches and the other a Church), the danger is here avoided of presenting an oversimplified story of these past five years. The selection of writings and addresses of these two men whose spirit and decisions had so much to do under God with the miracle of new relationships that have come to pass before our eyes in our own time among the Christian Churches, may be read with an eye to learning both the spirit and form that ecumenical progress demands. This book has not the unity of a single authorship or that of a book by an historian who, after the event, inductively constructs the meaning of the story. This is rather the material on which at some later time this history will be based. Just as the unity of the Churches today is a unity in the process of becoming and not that perfect eschatological unity true ecumenists work and hope for, so this book is a contemporary account of a developing and changing movement, the end of which in history is yet in God's hands.

Nevertheless, what is written here can teach us now how to be ecumenical in the as yet unknown but surely exciting years that lie before us. The first and most important quality of these ecumenical writings is the spirit in which they are written. It is a spirit which is neither romantic nor skeptical. It is neither naïve nor suspicious. It is neither polemic nor diplomatic. Nor is this spirit either optimistic or pessimistic in a secular sense. Rather, it is a spirit which is clearly derived from the life, teachings, death, and resurrection of the One who is at the center of Christian faith and at the same time the center of the ecumenical movement. It is the spirit of that mature brotherly love which is the authentic response of faith to the revelation of God in Jesus Christ centered in the self-giving sacrifice on the Cross that made available to man a new qualitative, demonstrative understanding of what love is.

Again and again in discussing the ecumenical movement, Protestants fall into the trap of speaking as if one became ecumenical chiefly because he was romantically naïve and optimistic or because he was trying in some political way to unify the Church against an increasingly secularistic world. This book makes it clear that, on the contrary, ecumenical motivations have risen and must arise out of that love for the Christian brother centered in Christ, which nevertheless is directed towards every man in the whole world without any limit whatever. This love is radically revolutionary not only in theology but also in ethics and ecclesiastical affairs.

The second quality of the ecumenical writings contained herein which can teach us all how to be truly ecumenical is that they make it evident that there is no contradiction between Christian love, so defined, and rigorous intellectual analysis combined with varied theological convictions. Some ecumenists suppose that the central tension of ecumenism must always remain between love and truth. These writings show that without love, truth is distorted, and that without truth, love is less than Christian.

The depth and breadth of the theological understanding of the co-authors of this book are revealed on every page. It is, however, a theology that is made alive in a sense that so often is not identified in academic theological faculties and seminaries by its true existential quality. These theological analyses and convictions have been forged in the heat of administrative decisions which, as we look back, were crucial if the ecumenical movement was to move forward. Every important position and counter-position here put forward in the general ecumenical debate amongst our Churches, as well as in the more specific debate about Roman Catholic ecumenism, was either decided on the spur of the moment or recognized as an important part of the agenda for the future. The troubling thing is that so much of the current debate is being carried on at a superficial level that often has not troubled to examine what has been already thought and done theologically, thus threatening to repeat the past instead of building upon it.

Let me conclude this Introduction by noting what seem to me the most important new questions that the ecumenical movement must grapple with if the movement is in fact to continue to move. I put them in the form of questions.

(1) How can the rank-and-file members of the Churches in the ecumenical movement become responsibly involved in the controversial issues of the movement so that its result is unity and not schism? Every Christian Church, including the Roman Catholic, faces this problem in sharp form. Some are so frightened by the prospect of new horizontal schisms among the Churches, that they counsel caution and consolidation rather than further risk by further advance. It is my growing conviction, gained partly from reading the history of the past in this book, that the issue remains not one of courage or timidity, taking risks or playing it safe, or success in manifesting ecumenical unity or failure in our efforts, but rather that the issue is between obedience and disobedience. The ecumenist is bound to hold high a standard of unity, renewal, and mission to which all Christians can rally; the outcome remains in the hands of God.

(2) How can the Roman Catholic Church find its way of co-operation and dialogue with the other Churches and the World Council of Churches in view of its size and its convictions about papal primacy, since these make its understanding of ecumenism so difficult for other Churches to cooperate in return and to speak in equality? The promulgation of *De Oecumenismo* was a tremendous advance for the whole ecumenical movement. In principle the other Churches must accept that statement as outlining the ecumenical stance of the Roman Catholic Church. Ever

since the Toronto statement of the Central Committee of the World Council of Churches we have understood that there is no single ecumenical ecclesiology. The Churches within the membership of the World Council of Churches differ deeply here from one another. But Pope Paul VI, in his recent statement to Cardinal Bea's Secretariat, pointed out the embarrassment that is inherent in the particular Roman Catholic conviction on the primacy of the Pope. He asked his ecumenical Secretariat and all the Roman Catholic faithful to make clear in all dialogue their loyalty to this conviction. This was a proper request. Dialogue which diplomatically conceals real issues is no dialogue in the sense that it is described in this book. It is not yet clear how serious an obstacle to ecumenical advance this unique claim to uniqueness, coupled with great size and power, will be. We may, however, be sure that it can be overcome in part in the kind of love and mutual concern that must remain the spirit of ecumenicity.

(3) How can the Protestant Churches move forward in their cooperation and dialogue with each other and with the Orthodox Churches and the Roman Catholic Church, without further alienation of those young men and "progressive" leaders in all the Churches who increasingly feel that the pace of the ecumenical movement is too slow, since in their view it is being strangled by the cautious official and institutional leadership of ecclesiastics? Roman Catholic *rapprochement* to the Protestant Churches is not nearly so much of a theological threat to the so-called conservative evangelicals as it is to the so-called progressive men and movements who are beginning to act according to their new motto: "No more consultation without implementation." We must add to this general mood the specific

theological questioning of the theological consensus by which a generation of the ecumenical movement has been guided. Under sharp attack are the unity and interpretation of Scripture, the transcendence of God and therefore the reality of the incarnation, and the traditional, personal, and social ethics of the Church.

I suggest that the ability of the ecumenical movement to continue to move will depend under God on there being found, at the least, provisional answers for these important questions. To study how the leaders of the ecumenical movement solved problems fully as great as ours in these last decades, is surely a good foundation for those who have these new problems to solve. *Peace Among Christians* is required reading for such a purpose.

Geneva, May 23, 1967

PEACE AMONG CHRISTIANS

I.

Vatican Council Ecumenical Report

BY AUGUSTIN CARDINAL BEA

EVEN THOUGH each of the first three Council sessions concluded on a more or less pronounced note of disappointment, and therefore of apprehension, the end of the Council was largely marked by joy and rejoicing. Nevertheless, we must try to look at this problem squarely and draw up a realistic appraisal of both joy and sorrow, of both negative and positive aspects of the situation, in the same way that the Council in many respects illustrated the double saying set forth in the Psalms: "He that goeth forth and weepeth, bearing precious seed," so it begins, "shall doubtless come again with rejoicing, bringing his sheaves with him." The Council, too, bore the Church's essential distinguishing characteristic which, in the words of St. Paul, has "this treasure in earthen vessels, to show that the transcendent power belongs to God and not to us . . . always carrying in the body the death of Jesus, so that the life of Jesus may also be made manifest in our bodies" (2 Cor. 4, 7. 10). In the midst of our well-justified joy for the Council's successful outcome let us not forget the difficulties and ordeals we went through, the most trying of which was undoubtedly the loss of the Council's creator, our beloved Pope John. The memory of these trials and tribulations should serve to remind us in the future, when encountering unavoidable difficulties in our coming ecumenical work, that God has, in the past, helped us to overcome all obstacles, and that he can therefore continue to help us in the future.

However, we must in all fairness duly emphasize the treasures which the Council has bestowed upon us—in particular, the humanly frail aspect of earthen vessels, as stressed repeatedly, though often a bit too much, by the press during the Council. We should and must humbly remember these treasures entrusted to the Church by God which were revealed anew by the Council. We must thank God for them and bear in mind the obligations which arise as a result of them.

The first of these treasures is the achievement, experience, and gradual improvement of the truly fraternal Christian atmosphere surrounding the separated brethren, above and beyond all which tends to separate them, and above and beyond all separations themselves. Let us put aside the theological bases of this fraternal attitude for now; they have been described solemnly and in detail in the *Decree on Ecumenism*. The only fact we must mention is that interest in the Council on the part of other Churches or Church communities increased steadily throughout the year to such an extent that the number of Churches and Church communities represented during the last Council period had risen to 23, whereas the number of delegate observers or guests at the Secretariat amounted to 103. This number had therefore more than doubled in comparison to the first Council period. I frequently spoke about this atmosphere during earlier world prayer octaves and on other occasions as well; but now there is additional evidence to this effect, namely, the testimony provided by the delegate observers themselves.

And this is not the evidence of a detached bystander, but rather that of an observer who publicly expressed his thanks, at the December 4th Council meeting, in behalf of all observer delegates and guests. Speaking about the delegate observers in the second person, he said:

"The welcome accorded you [observers] was an exceedingly warm one. Numerous gestures of respect, love, and friendship were made towards you. The word *dialogue* was not a meaningless one. You were given frequent opportunities to meet people and engage in conversations: and even though the bishops as well as the periti were overloaded with work, they nevertheless always took the time to acquire for themselves a clear concept of the beliefs of other Churches. The personal friendships formed during these years constitute the sort of riches which you will always bear with you."

Addressing himself to the other part of the audience, the same speaker was given the opportunity to offer evidence to the Council itself about the close participation of the delegate observers:

"The observers would like to take the opportunity to emphasize to the Council members that they partook in the Council's work not merely as parties interested from a distance only, but as true participants. What happens in the Catholic Church concerns other Churches as well. This insight was made gradually clearer during the course of the meetings. The Churches belong together in the name of Christ, above and beyond that which now separates them. The observers are convinced that the union established thus far can and will be strengthened."

We must certainly add to these comments the fact that what

has just been said applies not only to the Council and to Council conferences, but also to Church people themselves, in varying degrees and to varying extents. What happened in the Council not only served to form waves; it repeatedly carried over into new situations, and both influenced and formed the relationships between Christians of different Churches and denominations. Thus God used the Council as a tool with which to stimulate and promote this truly fraternal Christian atmosphere among Christians themselves. The greatness of God's act of goodness, as shown to us by means of this "ecumenical spring" (and with it the greatness of the gratitude we must offer Him) is shown in full when we compare it to the "ice-cold winters" which continued for so many centuries. The greatest thanks we can show for this blessing is to continue applying our efforts towards it, and preserve and improve this fraternal Christian atmosphere to an even greater degree.

The second treasure—an extremely rich and complex one—is composed of all the doctrines and insights of ecumenical importance which have been set down in various Council documents in the form of instructions and regulations. It is clear, on the basis of the unparalleled range and volume of the documents published by this Council, and on the basis of the fullness of their content, that it will take us a decade, even a century of continuous study and meditation, fully to appreciate the richness of this treasure. Here we are forced to content ourselves with merely a few allusions to the main issues. In doing so we are disregarding the *Decree on Ecumenism,* which has already been discussed within this framework.

First of all, we would like to mention the *Dogmatic Constitution on the Church*—and this must be mentioned due to the

40

fact that various subjects therein have been complemented by other decrees promulgated this year. What is of prime concern in this constitution, from an ecumenical point of view, is the part which explains the episcopate and the position of laymen within the Church. The Holy Father himself said that the First Vatican Council was complemented and completed by the Second, in particular as far as Church doctrines were concerned, and especially due to the fact that it is supplemented by the doctrine concerning the Pope's primacy which was promulgated at the First Vatican Council by means of an explanation of the doctrine on the episcopate and the nature of its spirit of fellowship. In order to show the significance of this doctrine from an ecumenical standpoint, it shall suffice to mention the position the episcopate occupied in the Christian Orient, and the role played by the alliance of the diocese with the patriarchates and autocephalic Churches. Furthermore, when one considers the extent to which the Pope's primacy is frequently equated with the most extreme type of centralization in the thinking of non-Catholic Christians, then one will also understand how important it was to the concept of unity when the Second Vatican Council clearly and solemnly proclaimed the doctrine that it was the assembly of bishops of the entire Catholic Church, with St. Peter's successor at its head, which represented the highest authority within the Church. Such participation on the part of the bishops in the government of the entire Church was to be further emphasized by the creation of the synod of bishops whose function it is to stand by the Pope in matters of gravity and importance concerning the world Church.

Another doctrine which has, so to speak, awaited clarification for centuries is the one concerning the position of laymen within the Church. We all know what a significant role laymen have played throughout various periods of Church history, and which they still play today in the non-Catholic Christian East and West. We are also aware of the tensions in this area which have frequently arisen in Church history. In order to give this subject the consideration it deserves, the Council, in the chapter of the constitution on the Church dealing with the People of God, first of all granted the same dignity and position to all Church members and summoned them to their calling towards holiness and the apostolic mission by means of the common priesthood. In addition, it clarified the distinctive position, rights, and duties of the clergy towards laymen. The apostolate of laymen was so important to the Council that it was dealt with later in a separate, very detailed decree.

No less significant from an ecumenical point of view is the *Dogmatic Constitution on Divine Revelation*. It is a known fact that this document is the one whose preparation caused tremendous difficulty. It is even more noteworthy that the document now promulgated is designated by the non-Catholic side as being the most important one emanating from the Second Vatican Council, ecumenically speaking. What, then, does this mean? To the extent that such a question can be answered within the narrow framework of this report, the following can be maintained: its importance lies in the fact that the fundamental problem was not attacked on the basis of any century-old polemic method of questioning (justified, though not as fruitful, as such methods may be); it was attacked in a concrete manner based upon the Church's awareness of its pastoral responsibility towards men. Then the following question was posed: What does divine revelation mean for the Church, and thereby for Christians, especially in the conditions they live under today? What, then, must Christians do in order to make proper use of this gift of God?

With this as their attitude, the Council, on the one hand, proclaims the Church's undivided love of the Holy Scripture on which its life is based: "The Church has always venerated the divine Scriptures just as she venerates the body of the Lord, since from the table of both the word of God and of the body of Christ she unceasingly receives and offers to the faithful the bread of life, especially in the sacred liturgy. . . . For in the sacred books, the Father who is in heaven meets His children with great love and speaks with them; and the force and power in the word of God is so great that it remains the support and energy of the Church, the strength of faith for her sons, the food of the soul, the pure and perennial source of spiritual life" (No. 21). It can therefore be concluded: "Easy access to the sacred Scripture should be provided for all the Christian faithful" (No. 22).

On the other hand, however, the Church emphasizes the function of tradition and of the teaching office: "Consequently, it is not from sacred Scripture alone that the Church draws her certainly about everything which has been revealed" (No. 9). "The task of authentically interpreting the word of God, whether written or handed on, has been entrusted exclusively to the living teaching office of the Church, whose authority is exercised in the name of Jesus Christ. This teaching office is not above the word of God, but serves it, teaching only what has been handed on, listening to it devoutly, guarding it scrupulously, and explaining it faithfully by divine commission and with the help of the Holy Spirit; it draws from this one deposit of faith

43

everything which it presents for belief as divinely revealed" (No. 10). He who is not only familiar with the age-old argument on the problem of Scripture and Tradition, but who is also familiar with the situation today, knows from these few words how to evaluate what the *Dogmatic Constitution on Divine Revelation* implies for the ecumenical situation.

It is hardly necessary to underline the ecumenical significance of the Council statement on freedom of religion. Just as it is absolutely necessary, in man-to-man relationships, for one human being fully to recognize the human dignity of another, and, indeed, respect it, it is even more necessary to do this in relationships between the various religions, and, most particularly, in interrelationships between the different Christian denominations. Convincing evidence of the significance of this problem is the fact that the World Council of Churches has dealt with it for years in conferences and in studies (from Evanston in 1954 to St. Andrews in 1960), up until the commission's corresponding report on "Christian Testimony, Proselytism, and Religious Liberty" was accepted by the Central Committee of the World Council of Churches in St. Andrews, and transmitted to the member Churches for their deliberation and reactions (see, on this subject, Augustin Bea, *Unity of Christians,* Appendix III). The reason why religious freedom in the different denominations is so important is clear: the mission entrusted to the Church by Christ, together with man's moral obligation to accept it, must, on the one hand, be proclaimed. On the other hand, however, such acceptance must unquestionably occur as a result of a freely made personal decision; faith must be admitted, exercised, and proclaimed out of free choice. All of these dictates, those of free exercise and proclamation, as well as that of free acceptance,

44

devoid of any external pressure or coercion, are equally important. It goes without saying that transformation of these dictates into action implies many different kinds of problems and tensions. It is therefore all the more important that the principle of freedom, at least as far as its main aspects are concerned, be made quite clear, so that we can put it into practice more easily, according to the given circumstances, and do so without infringing upon men's rights and principles. It is clear what the Catholic Church's distinct and solemn proclamation of its principles in this area means to ecumenical relations among the various Churches and denominations.

Finally, a word about the ecumenical significance of the *Pastoral Constitution on the Church in the Modern World.* Briefly: this constitution, from an ecumenical point of view, creates the widest possible basis for any future cooperation among Christians "in whatever projects a Christian conscience demands for the common good" (No. 4) and which the *Decree on Ecumenism* solemnly appealed to. Such cooperation among Christians "vividly expresses that bond which already unites them, and it sets in clearer relief the features of Christ the Servant." Through it "all believers in Christ are able to learn easily how they can understand each other better and esteem each other more, and how the road to the unity of Christians may be made smooth" (*Decree on Ecumenism,* No. 12).

The ecumenical significance and other implications of the doctrines and practical guidelines set forth briefly above can in no way be measured at this time. The Vatican Council itself provided the most shining example of true ecumenical attitude and action. This was simply, as we have already said, the fraternal meeting in prayer and work with non-Catholic delegate observers which was carried on on a daily basis. The meeting in prayer took place in a particularly touching manner at the combined divine services the Holy Father held with the delegate observers and Council Fathers on the afternoon of December 4 before the walls of the Basilica of St. Paul. Common services were conducted with active participation of the various non-Catholic observer delegates in reading and prayer. The Holy Father—to whose personal initiative the joint services may be attributed—not only recited the prayers on this occasion, but gave a stirring speech as well.

A second example, this one an illustration of true Christian love, was the solemn act whereby the Holy Father and the Ecumenical Patriarch of Constantinople, Athenagoras, declared jointly and simultaneously that they regretted and condemned the reciprocal excommunication of 1054, with all of its sad secondary effects, and removed it from the life and memory of the Church. It was not by mere chance that the entire Council's longest and most enthusiastic applause was given during this act, when the Holy Father and Metropolitan Meliton of Heliopolis, representative of the Ecumenical Patriarch Athenagoras, embraced each other at the Council meeting. This applause was proof of the extent to which the Council Fathers were aware of the absolute necessity and paramount importance of brotherly love in the sense of St. Paul's great song of love (1 Cor. 13).

In conclusion, we can say, while offering our deepest thanks to God, that He has bestowed upon us an abundance of His greatest mercy, both in an ecumenical sense and from the point of view of the Council itself. He has once again taught us to experience and exercise truly fraternal attitudes towards those of our brethren who are separated from us, and He has allowed us to establish brotherly contacts extending in all directions to such a far-reaching degree. In the Council documents He has shown us, both in theory and in practice, the way towards common love, prayer, and work with brethren of other Churches and faiths. These instructions are to be elucidated over and over again by means of additional guidelines which are to be set down in an ecumenical directorate. Furthermore, several committees composed of both Catholic Church members and their non-Catholic brethren already exist for the purpose of exchanging ideas on theoretical and practical subjects. Here I am thinking, for example, of the mixed committee created in February 1965 by the World Council of Churches and the Catholic Church, and in the one created in August 1965 by the Lutheran World Federation and the Catholic Church. Other similar groups are in the process of being formed; however, it would be premature to talk about them publicly. Moreover, commissions for unity are slowly but surely surging forth on the level of the diocese and on the national level; their function is to assume the work being carried out on the present level and direct it. These are all means by which to stimulate and foster such participation, which applies to all members of the Church indiscriminately, and which has been expressed as follows in the *Decree on Ecumenism:*

"Concern for restoring unity pertains to the whole Church, faithful and clergy alike. It extends to everyone, according to the potential of each, whether it be exercised in daily Christian living or in theological and historical studies" (*Decree on Ecumenism,* No. 5).

Thus, in this World Prayer Octave, we, too, wish to thank God sincerely for the great achievement which He has performed

47

through the Vatican Council in behalf of the ecumenical movement, and join with the Church in prayer: "*Confirma hoc deus quod operatus es in Nobis*": Strengthen, O God, that which you have implanted within us, within me, within all members of the one and only holy Church, of one mind and heart with His Son, to pray and work for this unity so that each man may take up his cross day by day together with Him, follow Him, and assume upon himself that which remains of Christ's afflictions for the sake of His body, which is the Church (see Lk. 9, 23; Col. 1, 24).

II.

Farewell Address to the Observer Delegates

BY AUGUSTIN CARDINAL BEA

DEAR BROTHERS in Christ!

I would like to thank your representative for the kind words he has just offered the Secretariat for Promoting Christian Unity in behalf of its activity. If you have been satisfied with your stay in Rome, with the manner in which you were able to carry out your assignment, which certainly could not have been an easy one, with the encounters and exchanges of ideas, then this is cause for great joy on the part of all of us here at the Secretariat. For this means that our efforts to make your stay and your work more useful and easier to carry out have been blessed by God, and consequently will be crowned with success, within the boundaries of the possible, of course. May the bestower of all that is good be thanked for this.

However, allow me quickly to add that our joy is derived much less from the success itself than due to the fact that you have been present here at the Council, and due to the variety of contacts which have been made, above and beyond the Secretariat, between yourselves and so many Council Fathers, and, finally, due to the fortunate contribution you yourselves have been able to make to the Council and to the ecumenical work of numerous bishops, which work is to be followed up during

the post-Council period. I have often spoken about your contribution to the success of the Council at receptions, in lectures, and
in various publications, and, in particular, I have spoken about
the ecumenical nature of this success, for which reason I have
no need to express myself on this point again. It shall suffice to
say that the very presence of the delegate observers and guests
of the Secretariat took on proportions that no one could possibly
have suspected as far as the number of observers and Church
communities and federations represented are concerned, and
from the point of view of the range and, so to speak, geographical universality of those represented. The meaning of your stay
in Rome extended far beyond your actual presence here, beyond
the study of documents, and beyond the contacts made with
those whose direct responsibility it was to work in this area.
Your stay always had deeper repercussions. We are well aware
of all of these things, but about a great many other issues only
the parties concerned are informed, or else these matters, for
some valid reason, remain hidden behind a veil of discretion, as
is imperative in such cases. But what we can state today is the
fact that we shall only gradually come fully to realize the blessing
the God of the Church has bestowed upon us in this domain as
time passes on. For this reason, we thank the Father of Mercy
for everything every day, and, most especially, on this, the day
of the Council's closing.

But, in all fairness, we must thank you, too, all of you who
have been indulgent, persevering, and kind-hearted supporters.
And, beyond you, I would also like to thank those who sent
you, the Churches, Church communities, and Church federations
whom you have represented and who represent you. Since human
thanks alone remain powerless, we shall direct our liturgical

prayer to God: "Lord, reward those who have been good to us with eternal life, for thy name's sake." In expressing our thanks we can perhaps also express the wish, or, if you please, the resolution that the experience acquired this year be carried on, and thereby, I dare say, develop progressively further in the future. During the course of this year we have all lived the words of the Psalmist: "Behold, how good and pleasant when brothers dwell in unity!" (Psalm 133, 1). We have discovered deep happiness in the feeling that we are brothers in Christ, and this, above and beyond that which separates us from one another, and in spite of such separations. We have also come to know how advantageous it is for all of us to meet fraternally in love of truth and in humility of love. But, as fruit of Christ's mercy, and consequently as a pure gift of God, this experience imposes heavy and imperious duties on us. I could almost say that it creates a new calling which is a modification of our traditional calling towards Christ, what I would like to describe as the ecumenical calling to dedicate ourselves to realizing the unity of the Church as desired and invoked by Christ, and as absolutely demanded by God. St. Paul's exhortation therefore applies to all of us: "I therefore . . . beg you to lead a life worthy of the calling to which you have been called" (Eph. 4, 1). In other words, we ought to live as our ecumenical vocation demands we live. I do not have to deal in detail here with the rich meaning of this fact. I would rather like to say that just as each human life, in accordance with its very nature, strives to create a new life, so must our calling seek to evoke other ecumenical callings, wherever we may go, whatever we may do, and kindle a new ecumenical flame in more and more hearts.

On this note, then, I would again like to thank all of you, and all those who sent you, and bestow upon you our most ardent wishes for your future endeavors, whatever they may be, and for the Churches, communities, and federations you represent. Let us hope that we shall have the opportunity to meet again when our work on the tremendous task common to us all requires such. But in any case, let us remain one with Christ, praying, working, taking up our daily cross with Christ, for the sake of His body, which is the Church (see Col. 1, 24).

III.

Reports to the Central Committee of the World Council of Churches

BY WILLEM A. VISSER 'T HOOFT

1. St. Andrews, Scotland, 1960

FROM EDINBURGH TO ST. ANDREWS

FROM EDINBURGH to St. Andrews is not a great distance, but fifty years is a long time and the Fathers of Edinburgh 1910 lived in a very different world, the world as it was before 1914 which seemed so incredibly stable. They did not foresee the cataclysmic series of events which began in 1914 and which has gone on ever since. It is easy to see that they had their blind spots concerning the world situation, though, as Canon Warren has reminded us, we should be especially humble about this in view of the possible verdict of 2010 upon 1960. So it might seem that there is an immense gulf between them and us and that we have little to learn from them. But as one reads the story of the conference one becomes impressed that in spite of the different environment, Edinburgh 1910 wrestled with some of the same fundamental problems that we have to wrestle with.

This becomes especially clear from the reports about the great and lively discussion at Edinburgh about coöperation and the promotion of unity. During the preparation of the conference the definite pledge had been given "that questions affecting the differences of Doctrine and Order between the Christian bodies should not be brought before the conference for discussion or resolution." For a number of missionary bodies (especially Anglican bodies) had made it clear that this was the condition for their participation. Now it would have been natural that because of this ruling, and because this was the very first time that concrete proposals for ongoing relationships between the missionary bodies were being discussed, the delegates would have concentrated exclusively on a discussion of practical cooperation in the missionary realm and would have carefully avoided the subject of church unity. As a matter of fact, the official report and Temple Gairdner's vivid account of the great debate show that more often than not the speakers expressed their conviction that cooperation was good, but that church unity is better. Twice the words are quoted in the letter published by the heads of Christian churches in Britain in 1906: "We agree in believing profoundly that our Lord Jesus Christ meant us to be one in visible fellowship." Bishop Brent pleaded for a truly Christian attitude to the Roman Catholic Church saying that in any scheme, practical or theoretical, for unity we must take into our reckoning that Church. There was a passionate plea for the creation of a united Church in China. And the need for a conference on questions "which have been tabooed at this conference" (that is, faith and order) was clearly affirmed. The tendency of the discussion is described by Gairdner when he says, "These words showed how naturally the idea of the Continuation Committee with its expected termination in an

International Committee on Missions, led the minds of the whole conference to contemplate the vision of a higher unity still."

It seems to me a remarkable fact that already at the time of the very first consideration of cooperation in the field of missions two things became so very evident, namely, that mission points to unity and that cooperation is not the goal, but a stage on the road to the goal. This means surely that if today we discuss the integration of two parts of the ecumenical movement, one of which has its first origin in concern for mission and one of which has its origin in concern for unity, we are not distorting, but fulfilling the intentions of the pioneers.

FROM CINCINNATI TO ST. ANDREWS

As we commemorate Edinburgh 1910, we must not forget Cincinnati 1910 and the beginnings of Faith and Order. We know the close connection between the two events. Bishop Brent came away from Edinburgh with the conviction "that the Spirit of God was preparing a new era in history." As he said in 1920: "It was the sense of God's presence at that conference and the wonderful and immediate results that led some of us to believe that a similar conference on matters of Faith and Order would be productive and good." Brent made his revolutionary proposal in a mass meeting on October 11, 1910. His force of persuasion and inspiration must have been quite extraordinary. For already on the next day Bishop Manning proposed a resolution to appoint a joint committee of bishops, presbyters, and laymen to consider this proposal, and one week later the very favorable report of that committee was unanimously adopted by the two houses. The resolution has often

55

been quoted, but introductory sections of the committee report are less well known. Here is a telling paragraph which has not lost its relevance: "With grief for our aloofness in the past, and for other faults of pride and self-sufficiency which make for schism, with loyalty to the truth as we see it, and with respect for the convictions of those who differ from us, holding the belief that the beginnings of unity are to be found in the clear statement and full consideration of those things in which we differ, as well as those things in which we are one, we respectfully submit the following resolution."

The proposal was unprecedented and it was not easy to get the churches to accept it. The man who did more than anyone else to convince the churches was Robert Gardiner of Boston, a lawyer who made the sacrifice of his time, his money, and his health in the service of this cause. It is a pity that the story of that devoted life has not been written.

Now it is remarkable that Faith and Order had a very clear awareness of the relevance of its task for the missionary cause. Brent himself wrote in *The Inspiration of Responsibility:* "We missionaries have moments of deep depression when the consciousness sweeps over us that it is little short of absurd to try to bring into the Church of Christ the great nations of the Far East unless we can present an undivided front. For purely practical reasons we feel the necessity of the Church's realization of unity. It must be either that, or failure in our vocation." Gardiner printed on all early Faith and Order pamphlets the full text of John 17, 21 including "so that the world may believe." And in later years Faith and Order voiced in its Constitution "the obligation (of the churches) to manifest unity and its urgency for the work of evangelism." Thus Faith and Order has been deeply aware of the deep relation between its concern and the concern of the missionary task of the church.

In the early days the great difficulty was to convince the churches that they were not going to be committed to decisions which they were not prepared to take. The original resolution had said that the conference would be "without power to legislate or to adopt resolutions." Later on this point was formulated in another way, namely that no Faith and Order conference should adopt any statement on a matter of faith and order unless it were approved unanimously, or at any rate without dissentient vote. Thus no church would be put in such a position that it had to withdraw from the ecumenical conversation. That is the basic reason why Faith and Order was careful not to formulate for itself a specific conception of the form which church unity should take.

Are we today in a different situation? That is a question which Faith and Order itself has discussed and which the Central Committee will also have to face. An inquiry held among a considerable number of church leaders has shown that there are still very different views about this matter. On the other hand, the Faith and Order Commission has unanimously adopted a statement on the nature of the unity for which we should work together. We face two temptations: the one is to force the situation by formulating a common goal representing the views of a majority. But this would be against the very principles of our movement as embodied in the Toronto declaration. The other is to be content with our present *status quo*. Our task is therefore to ask all our member churches to study the question whether in the light of the ecumenical conversation of the last ten or twenty years we can now say more together about the nature and form of the unity we seek than we have so far said.

In any case it is clear that in the coming years the work of Faith and Order must have a very considerable place in our life. The World Council can only be healthy if it accepts the basic dialectic in its life between that unity given to us in our present living together and that far more perfect unity which we are meant to have, according to the will of our Lord. That is why specific proposals on the future of Faith and Order will be submitted to this meeting of the Central Committee.

THE BASIS, 1910–1960

We have not yet finished with commemorations. For it was at that same General Convention of the Protestant Episcopal Church in 1910 that the formula which we have in the first article of the Constitution of the World Council was first used as a basis for an ecumenical undertaking. The resolution concerning the calling of a world conference on Faith and Order proposed "that all Christian communions throughout the world which confess our Lord Jesus Christ as God and Saviour be asked to unite with us in arranging for and conducting such a conference."[1] The question may be asked whether that Basis is not really much older and whether it does not come from the first World Conference of the YMCA in 1855. Bishop Manning, who had offered the original resolution, has said, however, that he was not aware of any connection between the two events. In any case, 1910 remains the date when this Basis

1. *Note:* This was the *second* resolution. The first resolution was the phrase: "which confess our Lord Jesus Christ as God and Saviour."

became operative in the ecumenical movement of the churches. In 1937, when the plan to create the World Council of Churches came before the Edinburgh Conference, Faith and Order stipulated that its work should continue to be founded on this Basis. It did not ask that the World Council as a whole should adopt the Basis for itself. But the Utrecht Conference of 1938 came to the conclusion that since this Basis had proved its value and had served to bring together churches of nearly all confessions, it should be proposed as the Basis of the World Council as a whole. And so until this day every church which applies for membership in the World Council is asked to state in writing its agreement with this Basis.

The discussion concerning the Basis which has gone on for fifty years, and which has unfortunately never yet been described and analyzed in a systematic manner, has been complicated by the fact that there is so much misunderstanding concerning the nature and function of the Basis. It is, therefore, important to ask what the Fathers of 1910 had in mind in framing it. In this connection the most important witness is Robert H. Gardiner, for he carried on the correspondence with the churches on the subject. A letter which he wrote in 1919 to Siegmund-Schultze seems to be specially revealing.[1] Gardiner wants to get in touch with the European churches and asks Siegmund-Schultze's help. He reports that so far none of the churches in Switzerland, France, Belgium, and Holland have been invited because it is so difficult to find out which of them confess the fact of the incarnation. He adds: "we believe that the idea of Christian unity is conceived by those who confess that fact and that doctrine in a way quite different from those

1. *Die Eiche,* April, 1921, p. 121.

who consider our Lord only as a great teacher of religion. Moreover we believe that the only hope for the future of the world is the visible unity which reveals to the world the incarnation of God in the person of His Son Jesus Christ . . ."[2]

This is an important statement, for it makes really three essential points about the Basis. The first is that the Basis is functional. Its first purpose is to determine which churches should be included in this fellowship. It does not say: this is all that we can say together, or this is our common denominator, or this is our minimum creed. It says: Jesus Christ, God and Saviour gathers us together. The Amsterdam message says the same thing very simply: "He has brought us here together at Amsterdam. We are one in acknowledging Him as God and Saviour."

The second point is that the Basis affirms the incarnation. However incomplete it is, it was meant to say: "God was in Christ" and in saying that to distinguish the Christian faith from any forms of humanism or syncretism.

The third point is that it means: we do not stand for some vague, undefined unity; the kind of unity we seek is that which is given in the fact of Jesus Christ. We do not want to mix up this unity of which Christ Himself is the author with secular or syncretistic concepts of unity.

It seems to me that Gardiner's conception of the Basis is very relevant to us today. There is much to be said for making certain additions to the Basis in the light of all that we have learned in half a century and a specific proposal to do this will be submitted to the Central Committee, but it would, to my mind, be a mistake to change the *character* of the Basis and to make it something else than what it is now, namely an identification of the nature of our fellowship and an orientation point for our com-

2. Retranslated from the German.

mon task. In other words, the Basis must in no way have the appearance of a series of what used to be called "fundamental articles" for the union of the churches. Its one and only purpose must be to say what holds us together in the World Council, what is the starting point of our conversation and the foundation of our collaboration.

RELATIONSHIPS WITH THE ROMAN CATHOLIC CHURCH

On this subject which has been treated at some length in the report of the Executive Committee I should like to make one further comment.

If I analyze the present situation correctly, the road which the World Council will have to find in this respect is the road between two abysses.

The one danger which we will have to avoid is that we should consider ourselves or become generally considered as an opposite number of or a counter-weight to the Roman Catholic Church. This is a real danger, for there are many Roman Catholics who *compare* the World Council with the Roman Catholic Church as if they were comparable entities, and there are those on our side who think too easily in terms of the formation of ecclesiastical power constellations. The natural Adam in us and the political categories which are current in the world can easily drive us in this direction. But that would be a spiritual disaster, because we exist to work for unity and not to replace a division between many groups by a division between a few large groups. We must, therefore, remind ourselves and others that the Council is a body *sui generis* which refuses to become the adversary of any church or group of churches, and stands for unity in Christ of all who recognize Him as God and Saviour.

On the other hand, there is the danger that in order to facilitate contacts with the Roman Catholic Church we should give up convictions and principles which belong to the very essence of our movement. In saying this I think particularly of the advice that a certain number of Roman Catholic ecumenists are giving us. This advice amounts to saying that the one and only valid activity of the World Council is theological study and conversation about the issues of reunion of the church. Everything else is considered by them as a dangerous deviation from the true task of the Council. Now we have made it abundantly clear that full unity is and must be the goal of the World Council, but we believe at the same time that there are urgent common tasks to be performed even now, and that the performing of these tasks will help us to advance towards unity. We come from Edinburgh and Stockholm as well as from Lausanne, and we are not ashamed of any of our ancestors.

There are other things in our living tradition which we are not prepared to give up for any price—our convictions about religious liberty, our concern for an ecumenical relationship between the churches in which there is a real listening to each other.

To avoid both dangers will take much wisdom and patience. But the purity of our cause is at that price.

REGIONAL DEVELOPMENTS

In each of the major regions of the world there are now regional ecumenical bodies which bring the churches together to deal with common concerns within the region. The East Asia Christian Conference is of special significance for us because of the close relations which it has with the World Council, and because of the fact that in 1961 the attention of the ecumenical movement will be focussed on Asia. It will hold a major meeting of its Committee just before the Council Assembly in India. The European Conference of Churches will hold its second meeting in October in Denmark; one of the services which it renders is to bring leaders of Western and of Eastern European churches together. The Latin American churches will hold a continental meeting in August, 1961, and have graciously invited the Council to be represented at that meeting.

In view of the dramatic changes which take place in that continent, we have reason to concentrate our attention especially on regional developments in Africa. We are glad that the All African Conference of Churches is in process of formation. The World Council has no official relationship with the Provisional Committee of the AACC but both the IMC and the Council have been in close touch with the leaders and have in recent months been able to discuss fully with its leaders in which ways the two world bodies can best help the African Churches in their new and formidable tasks. In particular, ways were discussed of strengthening the AACC and of providing better coordination, especially at the early stages of planning, among the many ecumenical initiatives now being taken in Africa. A working party under the chairmanship of Mr. Henry Makulu (our new staff member from Africa) will serve as a clearing house for this purpose. In this way we can ensure that any plans concerning Africa such as those in the realm of the study on rapid social change, the meeting of acute human needs and others concerning the training of leadership which will be submitted to the Central Committee, will be rooted in the life of the African churches themselves. In this connection it is encouraging and, we hope, symptomatic, that the applications for membership in the Council of five African churches will come before us in these days. We rejoice in the fact that precisely at this decisive period in the life of Africa, African Christianity plays an increasingly important role in our Council.

SOUTH AFRICA

I should also like to make a brief comment on the actions which the officers have taken with regard to the situation in South Africa. One of the most serious characteristics of that situation is the isolation of the churches and groups of churches from each other: there is a lack of communication between Christians of differing race or of differing language and between South African churches and the churches elsewhere. Our duty in this respect can be expressed in words used in a different context in the Council, namely the words of the Faith and Order Constitution: "to draw churches out of isolation into conference." The most significant moments in ecumenical history have been those at which Christians separated by seemingly insuperable barriers have struggled together to maintain their fellowship and to arrive at a common mind. We must work and pray for this purpose in South Africa as we have done in other situations, most recently through a CCIA constitution in Rhodesia.

There is need for such an ecumenical process not only between them but also between these churches and the World Council as a whole. We should have done far more than we have done to arrive at a deep understanding of the complex problems of human relations in South Africa. We must now do all we can to achieve this by unhurried consultation between a representative Council delegation and delegations of the South African churches. We will, therefore, have to be good listeners, but that does not mean that the role of our delegates will be a passive role. Our delegates will not be empty-handed when they go to South Africa. They will come with the convictions held in the ecumenical fellowship as most clearly expressed in the report of the Second Assembly at Evanston, and seek to represent the mind of the family of churches of the Council. Our hope must be that through such meeting of minds we will not only help to create more ecumenical fellowship between the churches of all races in South Africa and between them and the Council, but also and especially make a substantial contribution to the cause of justice and freedom for all races of mankind.

2. Paris, France, 1962

1937–1962

The plan to form a World Council of Churches took definite shape at a meeting in Westfield College, London, in July, 1937. It was submitted to and accepted by the Oxford Life and Work Conference in the same month. The Edinburgh Conference on Faith and Order took positive action on August 11th. So we can say that this meeting of the Central Committee takes place exactly twenty-five years after the day when the momentous decision was taken to create the World Council of Churches.

The action taken at Westfield College by the thirty-five who had been appointed by the Life and Work and Faith and Order movements was a bold one. It is true that there had been a good deal of discussion about the bringing together of Life and Work and Faith and Order. It is also true that Dr. J. H. Oldham, Archbishop Söderblom, and the Ecumenical Patriarchate of Constantinople had suggested many years earlier that a Council or Koinonia of Churches should be formed and that that idea had been mentioned several times in the ecumenical meetings of the thirties. But the idea had so far remained just an idea and no one had yet given it such definite shape that it could be submitted to the churches and the ecumenical bodies. The correspondence of the period shows how extremely uncertain the ecumenical leaders of the time were as to the next steps ahead. But during the three days at Westfield under the leadership of Archbishop Temple and Dr. J. H. Oldham there was a sudden crystallization and the remarkable result was that the meeting agreed unanimously to a very concrete blueprint of the new ecumenical body to be created.

The solidity of the work done in those days is proved by the fact that most of the features of the original plan have been maintained, and have become part of the constitution and life of the Council. The basic thought was, as William Temple put it: "Our whole movement can only exist so far as the churches take real responsibility for it." So they decided to plan for a Council which would be "representative of the churches." The Westfield Fathers were also the first to formulate the principle that the Council shall not legislate for the churches or commit them to action without their consent. They conceived the idea of an Assembly once in five years and an annual Central Committee. When they thought of an Assembly of 200 delegates they did not see far enough into the future. On the other hand, they expressed a conviction about the role of the laity which is very similar to what the laymen said in New Delhi: "The witness which the church in the modern world is called to give is such that in certain spheres the predominant voice in the utterance of it must be that of lay people holding posts of responsibility and influence in the secular world."

The plan was bold because it meant the creation of a body such as had never existed in the history of the church. It was also realistic in that it asked no more of the churches than a definite commitment to do what they had already begun to do in a less formal way. But the plan was based on the hope that this first step towards unity would lead to further steps. Writing a few months after the meetings of the summer of 1937, William Temple said: "It [the Council] will thus supply a measure of union in organization corresponding to our present measure of spiritual unity, and facilitate the growth of a deeper and wider unity, which may in time express itself in more perfect union" (*Christendom* 1938).

These words, "the growth of a deeper and wider unity," make us pause. Our unity has certainly become wider. The men and women of Westfield did not dream that the Council would grow so fast. Are we equally sure about the deepening of our unity? There are both encouraging and disquieting symptoms. Encouraging I would call the spirit in which we worked and lived together in New Delhi. Disquieting I would call the fact that we do not find in our churches a more active desire for a fuller unity. Now 25 years is a very short time in the history of the church. What counts is whether the unity we have is really leading to the more perfect union which the Lord has in store for us.

THE EASTERN AND WESTERN TRADITIONS IN THE COUNCIL

No other action taken by the New Delhi Assembly has been so widely discussed as the acceptance into membership of the Orthodox Churches of the U.S.S.R., Romania, Bulgaria, and Poland. In the press it has far too often been discussed in secular rather than Christian categories. On the other hand, there is reason for gratitude that in the vast majority of our member churches the true spiritual meaning of this event has been understood. That meaning is that the churches in Eastern Europe and the churches in other parts of the world feel after many centuries of isolation that the time has come to enter into fellowship with each other. No visitor from the outside coming to these churches can doubt that there lives in their midst a strong desire for fraternal relations with their fellow Christians in other parts of the world, and the action of the churches assembled at New Delhi showed that there is on their side a corresponding desire for fellowship.

In this way the question of the relationships between churches of the Eastern and churches of the Western tradition which has been an important issue in the life of the ecumenical movement since its beginnings has now taken on even greater significance and urgency. We are asked whether we will make full use of this great ecumenical opportunity. What is wanted first of all is that we should come to know each other far better than we have yet done. We should therefore welcome the exchange of visits such as those organized by the churches themselves. We are also glad that an increasing number of staff members of the Council are becoming acquainted with the Orthodox Churches. It is also helpful that we have now in Geneva, in addition to the representation of the Ecumenical Patriarchate, the representation from the Patriarchate of Moscow.

But information is not enough. What is required is a real ecumenical encounter in which the churches learn from each other, enrich each other, and explore together how they may go forward on the road to unity. We are therefore happy that members of two theological commissions of Faith and Order will soon visit the Russian Orthodox Church in order to engage in serious theological conversation with representatives of that church. We hope that in the forthcoming World Conference on Faith and Order, but also in the work of all other divisions and departments, we may help in breaking down the centuries-old estrangement between the Eastern and Western traditions so that they may share together the spiritual gifts which they have received.

In our own church-language "Eastern" and "Western" have a meaning which is totally different from the meaning which these words have in modern political language. We give priority to the question of the relationship of the Eastern and Western expressions of Christianity. But we know also that the coming in of a number of large churches living in Eastern Europe (to be followed by other churches if the Central Committee accepts the applications for membership which have come in recently) increases our responsibility for constructive action with regard to the ideological and political tension between the largest power-blocks. Our great advantage in doing this is that as Christian churches we share in our faith and we meet therefore as brothers in that faith and not as representatives of rival ideologies. We know that no cultural, social, or political ideology can be identified with the Christian faith. That is not to say that we find it easy to arrive at a common mind about the tough issues of international relations. But it does mean that, as has been shown in New Delhi and at the Disarmament Consultation under the auspices of the CCIA in Geneva, we can arrive at common conclusions about a number of important issues and thus make a common witness to the world. And though so far on such a crucial matter as the cessation of atomic tests our repeated warnings have not yet been heeded, we must not become weary, we must continue to speak out, we must combat the hopelessness and defeatism that is so widely prevalent and continue to believe that a clear testimony concerning peace and justice will finally meet with a response in the hearts and minds of men.

IN THE YEAR OF THE SECOND VATICAN COUNCIL

Within a few weeks the Second Vatican Council will begin. That Council will be of such great direct significance for a vast part of Christendom and have such important implications for the relationships of the Roman Catholic Church to all other Christian churches that we of the World Council of Churches with our concern for the whole cause of Christ in the whole world must feel in a very real way: *nostra res agitur*. Now it is at the present moment difficult to get a clear picture of the present position with regard to the preparations made for the Council. The information which has been given is of such a vague character that we can only have the most general impression of the proposals which will be submitted. Moreover we hear on the one hand voices which give the impression that the Council will go very far in the way of renewal and reform, but we hear on the other hand voices which do not only warn against too great expectations, but consider that no steps will be taken which will make for an appreciable change in relationships between the Roman Catholic Church and the other churches.

In these circumstances we must confine ourselves to the basic question which attitude the World Council should take to the Council. It seems to me that this can be formulated in four points.

In the first place, we must follow the Council in the realization that much is at stake for the cause which we serve. We should accompany it with our prayers, seek to be fully informed about its work, do nothing which can make the task of the Council Fathers more difficult, do everything that can encourage them in the accomplishment of the task of renewal of their Church. It is in this spirit that our Executive Committee has decided to propose that the invitation to send observers from the World Council of Churches to the Council should be accepted.

In the second place, we should make it very clear to our constituency what the present position is with regard to the relations between the Roman Catholic Church and ourselves. That position is simply that we seek to be well informed about each other and let each other know about our various concerns. There is no question of any negotiation about organizational links and of course even less (since this is clearly forbidden by our constitution) of the World Council acting for any or all of its member churches in this relationship.

It is true that something new has happened. Even a few decades ago it would have been considered unthinkable that Roman observers chosen by a Vatican Secretariat should attend a World Council Assembly and that the World Council should be asked to send observers to a Council of the Roman Catholic Church. But the new development, while important, represents a modest step and means only that it is believed on both sides that Christians should not remain in complete isolation from each other.

In the third place, it seems to me that we should make it very clear that on the basis of our ecumenical convictions we hope that a real dialogue may be established between the Roman Church on the one hand and the World Council with its members churches on the other hand. Should we speak of a hope when we find already so much conversation going on between Roman Catholics and churchmen of other churches and when the literature on this subject has become of such overwhelming dimensions? Yes, for it is one thing to have these useful conversations between individuals and it is another thing to have a dialogue between *churches*. What is called the new climate is not likely to have any permanent effect if it does not lead to a dialogue on the level of the churches themselves. In other words, we cannot and must not give up the hope that the Vatican Council itself will speak the language of dialogue. For just as there can be no healthy and, *a fortiori,* no Christian relationship between individuals where there is no dialogue, so there can be no constructive relationship between churches unless they are willing to enter into dialogue with each other. For what is dialogue? The great philosopher of dialogue Martin Buber gives a definition which I translate freely as follows: "Real dialogue takes place when each of the partners is really concerned with the others in their existence (*Dasein*) and in their particular character (*Sosein*) and turns to them with the intention that a living mutuality may be created." In other words, dialogue does not mean surrender of principle or conviction, or indifference to truth, but caring for the others, listening to them, desiring real communication and mutual enrichment. And this is *a fortiori* true for those who believe on the same Lord Jesus Christ. Father Congar has said that one of the most important principles of ecumenical dialogue is "to take seriously the questions which we address to each other." It is that type of dialogue which we need today between the Roman Catholic Church and the other churches.

72

In the fourth place, we must say that a dialogical attitude implies certain practical consequences. That is the reason why we are specially concerned about the action which the Council will or will not take with regard to questions which involve the relationships of the churches, such as religious liberty, mixed marriages, prayer for unity, and more generally to the question of the nature and limits of the Church. We must honestly say that even within the membership of the Council we have not yet drawn all the consequences from our relationship as churches engaged in an ongoing dialogue, and we must not ask from the Roman Catholic Church what we have not yet realized ourselves. But we are at least working out together a relationship in which each "looks not only to his own interest, but also to the interests of others" (Phil. 2). And we can and may ask that the unique opportunity of this Council, the first to take place since the modern ecumenical movement was born, may be used to show that the Roman Catholic Church realizes that churches which bear the name of Christ must, without minimizing their differences, demonstrate for his sake and for the sake of the world their true concern for each other and enter into a living dialogue with each other about the truth and the will of God.

THE MEANING OF "OIKOUMENE"

In his reflections on the New Delhi Assembly Father Beaupère has said: "Le Conseil œcuménique des Eglises apparaît comme un univers en expansion . . . Le Conseil œcuménique est maintenant 'un monde'" (*Parole et Mission,* avril 1962). He adds that this represents not merely a new stage but almost a transformation ("presque une mutation"). This is a true observation.

73

The pioneers of the Council wanted it to be a *World* Council, but in the early stages very large parts of the world remained unrepresented and therefore unable to make their contribution. At New Delhi we have made in this respect such a big jump that it is yet difficult to realize all the implications of the new situation. Through the integration of IMC and the Council, through the increase of membership in areas where we had few member churches, through the extension of our various services we are now in touch with churches in all major regions, the one important and regrettable exception being the churches of China. In many cases churches which are not members of the Council cooperate with us through missionary councils, regional or national councils, through the scholarship program, refugee work, or inter-church aid, through the Ecumenical Institute and the Theological Education Fund. And whatever else the New Delhi Assembly has meant, it has certainly given our movement a new realization of the world-wide character of the Christian church and of the impossibility to think of Christianity any longer in terms of one culture or a few continents.

Now this expansion of our horizons is in many ways exhilarating. We discover the dimensions of the work of God in the world; we come to see that the total life of the Church is of astounding variety and richness; we get an opportunity to share each other's burdens and to think of our own churches as part of a world-embracing *familia Dei*.

But there is also a danger. It is that we have now so many inter-church tasks, that we could forget the world outside the church. It would seem that just to get to know each other, to enter into theological conversation with each other, to render assistance to each other, to cooperate in the task of renewal of the church's life is already more than we can hope to accomplish in the coming years. It must be added that there is in many of our churches a sense of defeatism about their task in the world. So often the world lives and thinks and talks as if there were no church in existence. And the gulf between the intellectual and ideological forces shaping our civilization and the thought and witness of the church seems to be growing wider all the time. The temptation to take refuge in our own ecumenical world, where we have the great central convictions in common, is therefore a very real temptation.

But it is a temptation. For an ecumenical movement which would turn its back upon the world would no longer fulfill the purpose for which it exists. The very word *oikoumene* reminds us of this truth. Professor Werner Bieder has recently (in *Evangelische Theologie*) called attention to the fact that the passages in the New Testament in which the word *oikoumene* occurs, can be divided in two groups. In the first group *oikoumene* is used in the sense of humanity as it lives its common life in political or other communities and in its lost, unredeemed condition. In the second group the *oikoumene* is the world of men into which God intervenes by His act of grace in Jesus Christ and which is thus brought to its destination and end. An important example is Heb. 1, 6 where the New English Bible translates: 'When He [God] presents the first-born to the world [*oikoumene*], he says: Let all the angels of God pay him homage." Does this not mean that the risen and ascended Christ is presented to the *oikoumene* as its true Lord and that therefore the calling of the Church is to witness that all things are subjected to him (Heb. 2, 8) and that the "coming *oikoumene*" of which Heb. 2, 5 speaks is the whole wide world of humanity as it will be brought under His lordship?

There can then be no self-contained and introverted *oikou-*

mene. There can only be a churchly *oikoumene* which realizes that Christ is Lord and which must now carry that testimony in word and deed to the wider *oikoumene* which does not yet recognize what God has done for and in the world. It is in mission and service among men that we realize our ecumenical purpose. This is not to underestimate the importance of true unity. On the contrary, the issues of unity are so crucial because they affect the whole task of the Church in the world.

Seen in this light, our new study theme is just the one we need today. It speaks of the finality of Christ, that is, of his uniqueness and universality as the Lord of the Church, but it speaks at the same time of the age of universal history, that is, of the *oikoumene* in which it must be made known and manifest that He is the Lord of the world. As we seek to understand the full implications of those tremendous truths we will also see more clearly that the World Council of Churches must not only be a world-wide Council, but a channel through which the love of God is proclaimed and demonstrated to the whole world of men.

3. Rochester, New York, 1963

AFTER TWENTY-FIVE YEARS

In May 1938, that is, 25 years ago, the conference of church representatives at Utrecht asked the committee of fourteen, appointed by the Oxford and Edinburgh Conferences, to serve as the Provisional Committee of the World Council of Churches in process of formation. That meant that the World Council of Churches was no longer an idea, but, however embryonic, a reality. The Utrecht Conference realized that it had taken a decisive step. Archbishop Temple in closing the meeting said: "We have been led by the Holy Spirit; what has been achieved here is more than the doing of men."

It was indeed remarkable that it proved possible in such a short meeting of three days to reach unanimous agreement on the constitution of the new World Council of Churches which was to be submitted to the churches. This was due to the fact that a few men, very especially Dr. J. H. Oldham, Dr. William Adams Brown, and Archbishop Temple had prepared the ground so thoroughly and that the basic principles underlying the constitution had been worked out in the preceding years.

So the time had come to launch the ship. The ship was certainly not overloaded. Three and a half secretaries in Geneva and part-time secretaries in New York and London. A budget of some $30,000—a headquarters with nine rooms. And the storm was already approaching. While we met in Utrecht the League of Nations discredited itself in the matter of the attack on Ethiopia; a few weeks later the Munich crisis broke out; in the next year World War II began. Many international bodies collapsed or went into a long sleep. But somehow the World Council continued its process of formation and found itself increasing in inner strength and entrusted with increasing responsibilities. What was it that kept the infant alive? I believe that next to the grace of God it was due to a deep longing in the churches for a visible manifestation of the reality of the family of God as a fellowship created by the Lord himself. That longing received its answer as the Holy Spirit brought the churches together at the very time when humanity was torn apart.

ESSENTIAL ELEMENTS IN THE LIFE OF THE WORLD COUNCIL

The Utrecht Conference took or confirmed three fundamental decisions which have shaped the life of the World Council ever since and which are as relevant today as they were in 1938.

The first decision was to make the World Council a World Council of Churches in the strict sense, so that the churches themselves would control the Council and that the Council was their instrument of collaboration and fellowship. This decision has sometimes been criticized. Did it not mean the clericalizing of the ecumenical movement? Our answer is threefold. First, that only a Council which is rooted in the churches can help in accomplishing the main ecumenical task which is to give visible expression to the existence of the people of God united in faith, in witness, in service. Second, that there remains every opportunity for extra- or para-ecclesiastical initiatives and movements which desire to work independently. Third, that it is an old tradition in the ecumenical movement to make full use of the stimulus and inspiration of all Christian men and women, who have a specific contribution to make to the thought of the Council.

The second decision was to bring Faith and Order and Life and Work together. William Temple said at the time: "Much may be gained by drawing these together, for already the two movements have been led, by the logic of their own principles, to occupy the same ground." He added what was at that time a truly prophetic phrase: "And both will gain by seeing their special problems against the background of the church's primary task of world evangelization. In the year in which we have held the fourth World Conference of Faith and Order which has discussed from the angle of unity issues of decisive importance for each of our divisions, the year of the Mexico meeting of the CWME which will look at many of the same questions from the perspective of mission, and the year in which we prepare for a World Conference on Church and Society which will need the help of the men of Faith and Order and CWME for its theological and missionary aspects—in that year we realize more than ever that the move made at Utrecht was not merely a matter of organizational common sense, but also of profound understanding of the totality and cohesion of the tasks which the churches are called to perform in and through the World Council.

The third decision was to make the christocentric basis which had been the basis of Faith and Order the basis of the World Council as a whole. I believe that that decision was also of far-reaching importance. For it reminded ourselves and the world of the fact that there is a deep gulf between all forms of syncretism or relativism on the one hand and the universalism centered in Christ for which the Council stands.

THE DYNAMIC FACTOR IN THE WORLD COUNCIL

But the Fathers at Utrecht, or at least the most enlightened of them, knew that more was needed to make the World Council a truly dynamic movement. This is best illustrated by two remarks of our Honorary President, Dr. J. H. Oldham, which he made in a memorandum submitted to the Utrecht Conference. His first remark was that few churches had faced the fact that the ecumenical movement, if it is taken seriously, must mean that each church and each confession will subject itself to a self-examination in the light of the ecumenical confrontation. That was not written into the constitutional documents, but it is a truth which is essential for the life of the Council. Can we say that the churches have taken the ecumenical movement seriously in that sense and that the World Council has helped them enough to arrive at that profound self-examination? No one will dare to answer that question with a clear affirmative. The churches have learned from each other and they have been enriched through the ecumenical encounter, but the profound self-examination of which Dr. Oldham spoke is still a rare phenomenon. It is therefore important for us to hear that warning and to realize once again that the ecumenical movement will have failed in its mission unless it leads to that spiritual renewal without which unity will not be the unity in disobedience to our Lord.

Dr. Oldham made another very significant remark. He said that he was not interested in the Council as such, but in what it could do to equip the churches for their struggle to be the Church in the modern world. That reflection is even more important today than it was in 1938. As the Council has grown, in membership, in scope of work, in staff, in budget, as it moves into a more permanent headquarters, there is obviously a greater temptation to think of the Council as an end in itself. I do not think we need to give much attention to those who use the war-cry institutionalism about everything they do not approve of, but I think we should take seriously the wise words spoken in the report of Faith and Order's Committee on institutionalism. The authors of that report see quite clearly that institutionalism has its dangers. They say for instance about the development of religious bodies: "The second generation tends more to be concerned with consolidating efforts and with preserving power, including the structure of their own organization and the legitimacy of their office and status." But they make it very clear that the answer to the problem is not the rejection of institutions, but the right use of them. And they enumerate certain criteria in the light of which ecclesiastical institutions should be judged and adapted. Among these are self-criticism and renewal, ecumenical awareness, functional adequacy, coherence and diversification, sensitivity to recognized need. In other words, we have here the same point, this time in the language of sociology, which Dr. Oldham made at Utrecht. As we begin to consider again the structure of our Council, this then will have to be the constant question in our minds: Is the World Council the kind of institution which can help the churches in their struggle to be the Church, the witnessing, serving, reconciling Church in the modern world?

THE BEGINNING OF THE DIALOGUE BETWEEN EASTERN AND WESTERN CHRISTENDOM

Since its very beginning the World Council has been a meeting place of churches of the Eastern and churches of the Western tradition. It has therefore always had specific responsibility to ensure that after the many centuries of isolation from each other these parts of Christendom should enter into a real conversation with each other. But that responsibility has become greater now that nearly all major Eastern churches have joined the Council. It may well be that future church historians will judge the work of the Council in the 1960's from this particular perspective and ask: Did the Council really use the new opportunity to bring Eastern and Western churches closer together?

There are some encouraging signs. It is a fact of major im-

81

portance that the Orthodox churches have participated more fully in and made a more substantial contribution to the Montreal Faith and Order Conference than to any previous Faith and Order meeting. In this connection mention should also be made of a smaller meeting preceding the World Conference at Montreal which concentrated wholly on the fundamental issues which have arisen between Eastern and Western churches and led to a deep, honest, and always brotherly exchange of thought.

It must be said, however, that all this is only a beginning. The main task is still before us. And it is an immense task. We have to deal with enormous ignorance, with grave misunderstandings, with deep differences in the very categories of thought and expression. There is here work for scholars. But the scholars will not bring us much nearer together if they work in a vacuum. There is therefore equally the need for a new desire on the part of Eastern and Western Christians in general to get to know each other and to enter into a fellowship of mutual enrichment.

If we see this task in its true historical light—in the light of a separation that has lasted nearly a thousand years—we will approach it with patience. Western Christians will have to accept with patience that some of the conceptions which seemed to them to have become part of a generally accepted ecumenical consensus are called in question. And we must hope that Eastern Christians will be patient about Western impatience and see increasingly that such impatience is not based on a mere activism, but on a real desire for unity.

Both will have to accept the fact that the reality of ecumenical movement is not experienced in the same way by Eastern and Western churches. As we take up in this meeting of the Central Committee the question of the meaning of membership in the

World Council, this difference in outlook will have to be kept in mind.

The attitude in which we start this dialogue should, however, not be one of worry about the difficulty of the task laid upon us, but rather of gratitude that we belong to the generation of Christians who have the privilege of being called to take first steps in healing this very old breach which has had such tragic consequences for the life of the Church and for mankind.

RELATIONS WITH ROMAN CATHOLICISM

During the last twelve months another very important development in the field of ecumenical relations has certainly been the emergence in and through the Second Vatican Council of the clear desire of the majority of the Roman Catholic bishops to have their Church play a positive and active role in the ecumenical situation. The question of relations to other churches is only one of the many questions on the agenda of the Council. The Council is in the first place a Council for the renewal of life in the Roman Catholic Church and for the revision (*aggiornamento*) of its attitude to the modern world. And it may well be that this fundamental aspect of the Council will also prove to be its most lasting contribution to Christendom as a whole. For renewal in one church is always a challenge to other churches. But the Council is also dealing specifically with questions of inter-church relationships. No final decisions have yet been taken on this matter, but the discussions have already shown that a great change is taking place in this as in other respects.

Later in this session Dr. Lukas Vischer, who was the observer from the World Council at the Council, will report more fully on these developments. From the point of view of the general policy of the World Council, I should at this stage like to make the following remarks:

a) It is inevitable that at a moment of rapid spiritual change there should arise a certain amount of uncertainty as to the true significance of what has happened and is happening in and through the Vatican Council. It is therefore not easy to avoid either an overestimation or an underestimation of its significance. We must in any case not take the skeptical attitude which says that there cannot be a real evolution in the attitude of the Roman Catholic Church to other churches. Nor must we take the romantic line and speak or act as if the profound issues of faith and order between the Church of Rome and the other churches has been solved or almost solved. What we need is men who understand on the one hand that the Spirit is at work in the new self-examination and self-correction of the Roman Catholic Church and that all churches can learn from this, but who understand also that while this creates new opportunities for conversation and collaboration, the fundamental issues which have kept us apart remain stubborn realities.

b) The vital question at this moment is therefore not the question whether we can unite, but whether we can enter into a true dialogue with each other. And in order to have a dialogue we must agree on the nature of ecumenical dialogue between churches. It seems to me that real progress has been made in this connection, but that there is need for more clarity on this subject. I think of the fact that sometimes representative spokesmen of Roman Catholic ecumenism give the impression that all that is needed for the success of such dialogue is a different way of formulating the same positions. But is this sufficient? Should not real ecumenical dialogue always contain (to use the words of the Amsterdam Assembly) a process of "mutual correction" which goes beyond formulation? Again we believe that ecumenical dialogue must be dialogue based on the clear foundation of the common faith in Jesus Christ and we should like to be reassured that it is such dialogue and not a dialogue on the basis of some undefined general religious basis that is intended.

c) In the third place it seems to me that we of the Council must realize the fact that the Roman Catholic Church is now becoming an important center of ecumenical activities and initiatives. This is bound to affect the situation of the Council. Now we have never believed that the Council should have a monopoly *in ecumenicis*. Moreover this development is partly a result of the work of the Council, as authoritative Roman Catholic voices have stated. So, although at certain points this will make our work more difficult, we have reason to rejoice in the fact that the leaven of the ecumenical idea is at work in all parts of Christendom.

d) The existence of several centers of ecumenical initiative brings with it peculiar dangers and temptations.

One of these is that of looking upon the Roman Catholic Church and the World Council as two analogous and comparable bodies. It happens very often that in one way or another the advantages or disadvantages, the successes or failures of the Roman Catholic Church and the Council are set side by side. But this is a misleading procedure. For each must be understood in its own character: the Roman Catholic Church as a church and the Council as a council of churches. Each has its own specific task and must be judged in the light of that task.

Another danger is that there should arise a spirit of competition between two centers of ecumenical activity. This danger arises for instance when the impression is created that the Second Vatican Council is the most comprehensive center of ecumenical activity which puts all other previous ecumenical understanding in the shadow. Or when claims are made concerning the papacy, its world-wide role and its leading function in the whole of Christendom which the vast majority of non-Roman Catholics cannot possibly accept. Such utterances can only create reactions which will weaken rather than strengthen the new and still fragile relations which have been patiently established. On our side we must equally guard against utterances which could have the same effect.

Our role is not to compare or to compete, but to follow the specific calling to which the Council owes its existence. That calling is to bring all churches which are ready for this into a fellowship in which they seek to manifest through exchange in thought and life and through common witness and common service to the world that unity which they have already in their common faith in Christ and to prepare the way for the fuller unity which the Lord has in store for them. That task is so great, so challenging, and so largely unfulfilled that the World Council will have its *raison d'être* for many years to come.

e) Finally we have every reason to consider how in the new situation we may arrive at greater collaboration with the Roman Catholic Church in specific matters of common concern. Our relationships with the Secretariat for Unity have developed in an excellent way. It will of course largely depend on the outcome of the next sessions of the Council whether further steps should be taken and what these steps should be. But there is good reason to begin now to reflect on various possibilities. It seems to me that the following three lines of action are of special importance:

1. to create opportunities for discussion on theological and ecclesiological questions;

2. to create opportunities for discussion of practical questions such as the problems of religious liberty, of mixed marriages, relationships in missionary situations, and the issues of proselytism;

3. to create opportunities for discussion concerning the witness of the churches with regard to public and particularly international affairs.

REGIONAL DEVELOPMENTS

Now that inter-church bodies for cooperation have also been created in Africa and in the Pacific Islands we have come to the point that in nearly all parts of the world there exist regional bodies which are largely composed of our member churches. Latin America is an exception insofar as it has not yet set up a permanent organization similar to those in other continents.

These regional bodies are created by the churches concerned and wholly autonomous. Their value consists precisely in that they are rooted in their respective regions, that they are not controlled from the outside and that they can therefore deal with the specific problems of their regions or continents from the inside.

Thus they are also able to bring to the total world-fellowship an authentic expression of the convictions and concerns of the churches in their part of the world.

At the same time, the existence of regional bodies facilities the work of the Council in that they provide channels for communication and action for the Council programs. No two regional bodies have exactly the same relation to the Council. Some are more closely related to the Council than others. But all are in fact cooperating in varying ways with our divisions and departments. And all consider themselves as part of the total ecumenical movement and as fellow-workers with other regional bodies and with the Council in the total emumenical cause.

During the coming years we will have to give careful attention to the working out of our relationships with the regional bodies. We will have to consider how these relationships can be adjusted with our relationships with member churches and national councils. Plans have also been made for a consultation between representatives of confessional organizations and regional bodies. In our approach to these questions we are motivated by gratitude for the fact that in a world of great inter-continental tensions we find in our fellowships such strong bonds of mutual confidence between the regional families of churches.

CONCLUSION

Everyone who bears responsibility for the life of the World Council must wonder whether at such an early stage in its life it will be able to cope with the multitude of opportunities, tasks, problems with which it is confronted. Who could have believed in 1948 that the ecumenical development would be so fast and so full of unexpected happenings?

At such a time we must remind ourselves that this very development shows that we do not control history. History is in the last analysis a mystery, and church history is a particular mystery within that general mystery. We have not consciously created this present ecumenical situation. We have been led into it. We have been used for purposes larger than we had in mind. We may therefore believe that, if we are his faithful servants, the Lord of history will give us the wisdom and strength which we will need in order to be used for the accomplishment of his great design.

4. Enugu, Nigeria, 1965

THE SPIRIT OF THE PIONEERS

This is the time to remember the pioneers of the ecumenical movement, the men who had the spiritual imagination and the courage to create the movements which joined their forces in the World Council of Churches. For Bishop Brent, the father of Faith and Order, was born in 1862, Dr. John R. Mott, the father of the International Missionary Council, in 1865, and Archbishop Nathan Söderblom, the father of Life and Work, in 1866. Each of them had his own background and calling. Brent, the Anglican; Mott, the Methodist; Söderblom, the Lutheran: Brent pastor, missionary, and fighter against social evils; Mott layman, evangelist, and Christian strategist; Söderblom theologian, church-leader, and peacemaker. But they had also a great deal in common. And what they had in common is a precious part of our heritage. I would mention especially four aspects of their life-work.

(1) They were men with a truly catholic concern for the life of all the churches. Some of us remember that Mott used to speak of the spiritual debt he owed to all churches and particularly to the Orthodox Churches and to the Quakers. Mott and Söderblom were both leaders of the historic meeting of the World's Student Christian Federation held in 1911 at Constantinople which was attended by many representatives of the Eastern Churches, including the Rev. Germanos Strinopoulos, later Archbishop Germanos, Exarch of the Ecumenical Patriarchate and one of the first presidents of the World Council. The meeting was described as the first one at which the ancient Eastern Churches were brought in touch with the emerging ecumenical movement. Brent who had worked in the area of the younger churches made his contact with the older churches in 1920 when the Orthodox delegation came to the preliminary meeting of Faith and Order in Geneva, and wrote at that time: "We of the West need the fragrant, graceful worship of the East." All three had a capacity for appreciating genuine Christian faith in members of other churches. Söderblom surprised a sophisticated American dinner audience by giving a solo performance of the Sankey hymn: "There were ninety-and-nine," but he was also the man who did everything possible to bring Orthodox delegations to the Stockholm Conference. Brent felt at home in the evangelical atmosphere of the Edinburgh Conference of 1910, but tried also his very best to interest Roman Catholic bishops and theologians in Faith and Order. Mott used the same language in addressing the first sobor of the Orthodox Church of Russia in 1917 as he did in speaking to the

World Conference of Christian Youth in Amsterdam in 1939.

(2) So they refused to let themselves be imprisoned in any one particular section of church life. Brent played his great role in the Lausanne Faith and Order Conference, but participated with equal energy in the World Missionary Conference in Edinburgh and in the Life and Work Conference in Stockholm. Mott was of course involved in all ecumenical movements: founder of the World's Student Christian Federation and the International Missionary Council, presiding officer at the Oxford Life and Work Conference, chairman of section in the Edinburgh Faith and Order Conference, honorary president of the World Council of Churches. Söderblom was not only the soul of Life and Work but an active leader in Faith and Order.

(3) All three had a passionate concern for unity, but that concern was not for unity for its own sake. They sought unity for the sake of the fulfillment of the Church's mandate in the world. Brent and Mott emphasized especially the missionary motive. Söderblom proclaimed in the midst of the First World War that the unity of Christians should be realized in order that the Church could be the conscience of the nations. They were at one in setting the question of unity in the wider setting of the Church's calling and mandate in and to the whole needy world.

(4) All three stood for the renewal of the life of the Churches. They saw the need for a new obedience in a new situation. And so they sought to create new structures for new tasks. They knew that unity does not come by the addition of existing institutional forms by the common response of the churches to the Holy Spirit and their common transformation. Mott sought to "liberate the lay-forces," as he called it, and appealed to the

churches to take their missionary task seriously. Söderblom asked whether the churches must sit fearfully in their houses without faith and without courage and called them to discover together their prophetic ministry. Brent wrote during the First World War: "The world is falling to pieces, the churches are tugging behind the armies, and nothing is being done that is worthy of the name of witness-bearing for unity as Christ begs us to interpret it."

FOUR CRITERIA

We are not called to imitate these pioneers in every respect. But these elements of their work and message: true catholicity, dedication to the whole task of the Church, unity for the sake of the Church's mission in the world, readiness for a renewal of life, these remain part and parcel of the life of the World Council. And in these four respects we have yet far to go.

True catholicity. We have reached a point in the membership of the World Council at which our catholicity has deeply impressive possibilities. But it is still a potential catholicity. It has yet to be worked out and applied in the life of our churches. We shall only be truly catholic if we arrive at such a caring and sharing that the churches of East and West, of North and South, the young and the old, the small and the great, bear each other's burdens and expect eagerly to receive spiritual gifts from each other.

Dedication to the whole task of the Church. The World Council's work now covers many areas and concerns, but there are as yet too many people in our churches who are only for the specific concern of one particular division or department and too few who seek to understand and support the whole and who realize that it is only in their togetherness that our various types of work reflect the calling of the Church.

Unity for the sake of the Church's mission to the world. Here again we have a new opportunity since the integration of the World Council of Churches and the International Missionary Council. But the real task is still before us. We have only begun to ask what it means that the Church is called to mission and service in six continents and that the local congregation must have a missionary and not merely a conserving structure.

Readiness for renewal of life. Renewal means change and change means the giving up of patterns and structures which are no longer able to meet the need of the hour. It is therefore to be expected that there will always be tension between those who stand for renewal and those who would maintain existing structures. And it is not a foregone conclusion that every proposal for renewal is necessarily right. What is needed is that this tension be accepted as a constructive tension and that it does not lead to a hardening of opposite positions. The World Council must be willing and able to live with that tension in its own life. As a World Council of *Churches* it takes the existing structures seriously; as an ecumenical movement it must also stand for that renewal which is the condition of advance towards unity.

SOLIDARITY IN AN INTERDEPENDENT WORLD

One of the most important items on the agenda of this meeting of the Central Committee is the preparation of the World Conference on Church and Society which we hope to hold in 1966.

The World Council has always been concerned about social and international questions and they have had an important place in our deliberation. But this will be the first time since the creation of the World Council, in fact the first time since the Oxford Conference on Church, Community, and State in 1937, that we will have a large world conference specifically devoted to these issues.

It is not difficult to see why we need such a confrontation. There have always been social problems, but in our time the basic problem of overcoming hunger or poverty and of social justice has become the issue which dominates all other issues and on the solution of which the future of mankind depends. The interdependence of our modern world, the conviction that the needs of all can be met, the emergence of a new sense of dignity and a new hope among underprivileged masses, the emergence of so many new nations which desire to build healthy national societies—all these have made the international, intercontinental social problem the most inescapable issue of our time. As we meet in Africa many of us will be made even more conscious of its reality than we were before.

Now the Christian churches have a very specific responsibility in this field. They live in all these societies. They want to bear their burdens and to share in the task of nation-building. They are, through their work of mission and service, already deeply involved in the attempt to meet the most crying needs of the developing nations. But they know also that more, far more, is needed, namely, a great awakening of the spirit of human solidarity so that new structures of international and economic cooperation may be created and a concerted attack may be made on hunger and poverty.

So the question is firstly a spiritual question. Are we our brother's keepers? The question of my neighbor's bread is not a material but a spiritual question, said Nicolai Berdjaev. The secret of solidarity is the secret of men living together as fellow-creatures and brothers for all of whom Christ died.

Very many people have not yet understood the gravity of the responsibility which our generation bears in this respect. It is disquieting that in many countries the reaction to recent political developments has been to decrease rather than to increase the willingness to participate in plans for international assistance. Even in our own churches we have not yet created that awareness of the needs of other peoples and that readiness for large-scale and costly action without which no real advance is possible. Our World Council must show the way, not allow the tension between rich and poor to become an unbridgeable chasm, and help the churches to work for the revolutionary change in thought and action by which we can overcome social and national egoism and establish genuine solidarity between the peoples.

The world Conference on Church and Society can and must become an important step towards that goal.

RELATIONS WITH THE ROMAN CATHOLIC CHURCH

When I turn next to the relations between the World Council of Churches and the Roman Catholic Church I must begin by saying that I find it this time more difficult to speak on this subject than on any previous occasion. The reason is, of course, that recent developments, particularly those in the last days of the third session of the Vatican Council, have created a sense of great uncertainty.

On the one hand, we cannot and must not underestimate the strength of the movement for a true spiritual renewal which is at work in the Roman Catholic Church, and which has found expression in many of the speeches and some of the actions of the Council. We know by experience that there is a great difference between the wish for renewal and its actual application in daily church-life. But we must rejoice that there is so much new thinking, so much readiness to face anew the issues of the task and message of the Church in the modern world, and that this new approach is to such a large extent inspired by a new listening to the biblical witness.

On the other hand, we find that this renewal meets with powerful opposition in leading ecclesiastical circles. This has happened especially with regard to a number of matters which are of great moment for inter-church relationships. The result so far is that while in certain respects the Council has come to decisions which from an ecumenical point of view are constructive, it has postponed decision on other important matters, such as religious liberty, and in some cases only reaffirmed the old positions.

The question now arises: What should be our attitude at this time when there is reason for both expectation and disappointment? It seems to me that we ought to keep in mind the following considerations:

First of all we cannot forget that in our own churches we have by no means solved the problem of the tension between the forces of renewal and the existing structures.

Secondly, just as many Roman Catholics and members of

other churches rejoice together when they see in each other's churches signs of genuine spiritual renewal and are thus brought into a new relation to each other, so the anxiety about developments which put obstacles in the way to renewal is an anxiety in which many Roman Catholics and many Christians of other confessions share, so that there is a sense of being involved in a common cause.

Thirdly, the adoption and promulgation of the *Decree on Ecumenism* creates a new situation. It means that the Roman Catholic Church is no longer standing apart. It expresses its desire to enter into fraternal relations with other churches. It does so on the basis of a conception of ecumenism which differs in important respects from the conceptions of ecumenism held in our midst, but the fact remains that it desires to enter into conversation with other churches since it recognizes that in those churches Christ is working.

Now this surely means that the Roman Catholic Church and the non-Roman Catholic Churches bear a great responsibility for each other. Through the developments of recent years they have become more than ever "their brother's keepers." Is it not already clear that we have in fact exerted a great, as it were, subterranean influence upon each other? Has not the ecumenical movement been an important factor in the new development in the Roman Catholic Church? And have we not received important spiritual stimulation from the Roman Catholic ecumenists? Or if we look at the world situation, is it not clear that we are together faced with the obligation to reinterpret the task of the Church in an increasingly secularized world and to find the prophetic word to remind men in their disorder of the order of God? A mere polite and passive co-existence is not

97

enough. There must be the acceptance of responsibility of each other and therefore an intensive conversation. Is it necessary to say that such a conversation does not mean that deep convictions will be silenced or minimized? Insofar as this dialogue has to do with the specific issues of doctrine, it will of course take place between the Roman Catholic Church and other churches. From the point of view of the World Council it is normal and necessary that such inter-church discussions shall take place, if and when the churches are ready for them. Insofar as the dialogue has to do with matters in which the World Council itself is competent, the dialogue can take place between the Roman Catholic Church and the World Council. Our task is to work out a clear distinction between these two types of dialogue.

THE SIGNIFICANCE OF REGIONAL ECUMENICAL DEVELOPMENTS

A word should be said about regional ecumenical developments. During these last few years the process of bringing together the churches on a regional level has made much progress. It is noteworthy that now that such a development is also under way in Latin America, regional bodies exist in practically every continent.

But the significance of these regional organizations for the life of the ecumenical movement is not always understood. Thus it has recently been suggested that their growth is a sign of the disintegration of the ecumenical movement. Such a view reveals a great ignorance of the motives and factors which operate in this field. As the World Council seeks to promote the growth of regional bodies it is not digging its own grave. On the contrary. Ecumenicity begins at home; in the *oikos* of the churches.

But today when continents become realities in a way which was not true in the past, when they face specific common problems which differ from those of other continents, continental councils become an important link in the total ecumenical chain. Their first task is to serve the Christian churches in their own region and continent. They help the churches to solve problems which must be solved on a regional level. They can be the spokesmen of the churches to the various governmental regional organizations. As an example one thinks of the very important role which the All-Africa Conference of Churches has to play in relation to the planning of new structures for education in Africa.

But they can also render a very great service to the World Council. They bring to it the voice of their continent. One thinks of the very great significance of the plans made by the East Asia Christian Conference for the conference on "The Confession of the Christian Faith in Asia Today." They call the attention of the World Council to the specific needs of their areas. And they can act as channels for communication and action for the World Council. Thus the large "Ecumenical Program for Emergency Action in Africa" has been worked out in consultation between the WCC and the AACC and its success will to a large extent depend on the establishment of close cooperation between the two.

There is no desire on the part of the WCC to interfere in any way with the autonomy of the regional bodies, for it is by its very structure and constitution forbidden to do so. But we have a strong desire to work out relationships of cooperation with all regional bodies which are willing to cooperate with us.

5. Geneva, Switzerland, 1966

THREE TIMES GENEVA

In the ecumenical movement Geneva is known, if not always favorably known, as the place where the professionals of the movement carry on their multifarious activities. But as the Central Committee meets for the first time in Geneva it is fitting to remember that long before any headquarters of the three parent bodies of our World Council came to this city, Geneva served as the launching site of these bodies. This happened in 1920. Within one month three separate meetings were held. The Continuation Committee of the Edinburgh World Missionary Conference met at the Château de Crans, not far from Bossey. Under the leadership of Dr. Mott and Dr. Oldham it was decided to create a permanent organization which became the International Missionary Council. A few days later in the Hotel Beau-Séjour a preliminary meeting was held to consider the holding of a Universal Conference on Life and Work. Söderblom was the dynamic leader and invited the conference to meet in Uppsala. A committee of arrangements was set up. So Life and Work was launched. On the following days a preliminary meeting on a World Conference on Faith and Order was held at the Athénée. Here Bishop Brent and Robert Gardiner were the inspiring leaders. It decided on a plan for permanent organization and set up a representative committee to prepare for the World Conference. Faith and Order had thus become an inter-church, international movement.

Three different ecumenical bodies had been started at one and the same time at one and the same place. A few leaders attended two of the three meetings, but no person attended all three meetings. Each had its own ethos, its own sense of vocation, its own strong leader. There seemed to be little chance that these various enterprises could ever coalesce. But some voices were already heard which pointed to a future in which the separation would be overcome. At the missionary meeting Dr. Oldham said that "the international missionary organization would probably before long have to give way to something that may represent the beginnings of a world league of churches." At the Life and Work meeting Archbishop Söderblom, when receiving Archbishop Germanos and other Orthodox representatives, held in his hand the Constantinople encyclical which had been issued that same year and which had proposed the formation of a *Koinonia* of churches and in the drafting of which Germanos himself had played a decisive role, and compared this plan with his own proposal to form "an Ecumenical Council representing Christendom in a spiritual way." And at the Faith and Order meeting Prof. Alivisatos (the only member of our committee whose record goes back to 1920) also called attention to the proposal of the Ecumenical Patriarchate.

But it took a long time before the movements and the churches were ready for the establishment of an integrated council created by and dependent on the churches. And when the plan was at last adopted the world war made the postponement of its realization inevitable.

After the war a new beginning had to be made. Very real and deep contacts had been maintained, but nobody knew what shape the ecumenical movement would take after the end of hostilities. The Provisional Committee was called together in January 1946 in Geneva. We met, as we do today, in a new

building. Then it was at Malagnou and we were very proud of it, although the meeting suffered from lack of living room. But how happy we were to be together again, not least because, owing to the Stuttgart declaration of 1945, we were more truly united than ever before. Dr. Boegner said in his closing speech: "To have affirmed that our ecumenical communion has been maintained and even strengthened through all the suffering of these recent years will, I am certain, remain with us as one of the most unspeakable joys which God has given to us." It was a remarkably creative meeting. One of its notable aspects was the active participation of our Chinese brethren whose absence in our meetings of these last years we deplore so deeply. Approval was given to the setting up of the Department of Reconstruction, of the Youth Department, of the CCIA, and of the Ecumenical Institute. The year 1948 was chosen for the first Assembly. So Geneva had once again become a launching-site for the journey into ecumenical space.

This look at two crucial meetings held in Geneva is not merely of historical interest. It is at the same time a reminder that it is of the nature of the ecumenical movement to make new beginnings, to start out on new adventurous journeys. Today such a new beginning is required for other reasons than in 1946. We have reached the end of one period and the beginning of another because practically all the main confessional families have now accepted in principle that they have an ecumenical task to fulfill, and the churches in all parts of the world participate in that task. This means surely that from now on our chief concern must be to deepen rather than to broaden the ecumenical movement. The main task is now the task of concentration rather than the task of expansion. We have gone a long way in bringing churches together in a relationship of cooperation, of solidarity, of dialogue. If our staying together is not to mean to "stay put," but to "grow together," we will have to intensify our relations, to remove the obstacles to full fellowship, and to take concrete decisions about unity. That is why we have taken this time as our main theme: "The Ecumenical Way and the Specific Role of the WCC." We want to reflect on the new tasks arising in the new ecumenical situation. We hope that Geneva will once again be the launching site for a new journey towards new horizons.

ACCORDING TO THE SCRIPTURES

I should like to call attention to another lesson we have learned in the Ecumenical Movement, namely, that its health depends on the place it gives to the Holy Scriptures in its life. Already in 1926 Adolf Deissmann said at the Life and Work meeting in Bern: "The secret of the force of the Ecumenical Movement is to be strongly rooted in the Holy Scriptures." In the following decades that truth was strongly confirmed. For the drawing together of the churches in the thirties and forties, the finding of so much common ground at Oxford, Edinburgh, Amsterdam could not have happened if in those years there had not been a renaissance of biblical theology in so many different places and if that theology had not produced a remarkable consensus on many essential points. It was affirmed with remarkable unanimity that, although the Bible was a collection of writings of great diversity, as critical scholarship had shown, it was at the same time characterized by a strong unity in that it is the record of

103

God's redemptive activity of God in history having its center and goal in Jesus Christ.

It is this same basic conviction which has given its substance to the dialogue between Roman Catholic and other theologians. The secret force driving us together has been the biblical kerygma that we have heard again in a new way on both sides.

It is interesting to note that the first to draw the obvious consequence that common bible study should therefore have its regular place in ecumenical meetings were the youth movements. The World Christian Youth Conference of 1939 is especially memorable for this. And we have seen in many later meetings that the Bible is and remains the reliable link between us and the force that obliges us to enter into deeper unity with each other. So when in New Delhi we added the words "according to the Scriptures" to our Basis we were not simply making a pious gesture, we were recognizing with gratitude what we owe in fact to the Bible in our common life.

I believe that we have every reason to keep this experience in mind. For we have entered into a period in which what seemed to be abiding results of biblical scholarship are radically questioned and in which there is deep division of opinion among biblical scholars, very often of scholars belonging to one and the same confession. One of the basic issues has again become whether there is any really substantial unity in the biblical message.

Now it is quite normal that each generation raises new questions and that it has to work out its own consensus, but when we find that one of our most central common convictions is challenged we cannot remain indifferent. We have to say clearly whether we stand by that conviction. Can the words "according to the Scriptures" mean anything else than "according to the Scriptures conceived as a coherent whole and speaking with a common voice"? Much is at stake. To deny the unity of the Bible is to deny the necessity of the unity of the Church. A Bible interpreted as a collection of miscellaneous Christologies and ecclesiologies can hardly be the foundation of our calling to unity. Our movement can only be a dynamic movement towards greater unity, if we listen together to the one voice which gives us our marching orders. Fortunately, the Word of God has its own way of breaking through human misunderstandings. As the statement of the 1949 ecumenical meeting on the interpretation of the Bible said: "The Bible itself leads us back to the living Word of God."

THE OFFICE OF THE WATCHMAN

In these days we remember especially Archbishop Söderblom's unique part in the creation of the ecumenical movement. He had found it intolerable that at a time when the whole world was going through a catastrophic crisis, and millions of men went through unspeakable suffering, the churches were unable to render a united witness and so to help the world to find a better way than the way of self-destruction. He pleaded with the churches to speak out with one voice so that the demands of the Christian conscience might be clearly declared. If the churches would form a fellowship and speak out together in the name of their common Lord, he said, it would again become clear "that the Gospel is salt and fire and light."

As the churches began to respond to this task they found that they had in the first place to elaborate common theological and ethical positions. So Stockholm 1925 could not go much beyond declarations of principle. Oxford 1937 went further in the direction of concrete statements. By that time a larger number of Christian laymen had been brought into the movement and they helped greatly in ensuring that what the conference said was positively relevant to the realities of political and social life.

But it was only after the Second World War that through the setting up of the CCIA and through the work of the Department on Church and Society it became possible to follow international and social developments in a continuous fashion and with the necessary competence. In the meantime many churches have also come to the conclusion that it is not enough for the Church to speak out in general terms about peace and justice and that it is their duty in critical situations with grave moral implications to become specific to the point of indicating in which direction the nation or nations should go. It is most striking to see how in many countries the word of the churches has become an important factor in the formation of public opinion and in the making of national decisions about national or international issues. Some obvious examples are the hotly debated memorandum of the Evangelical Church of Germany about the relations of the German and the Polish peoples, the statements of the churches in Rhodesia and of the British churches about the unilateral independence of Rhodesia, the resolutions of the American churches about Vietnam, the report of the Netherlands Reformed Church about atomic weapons.

The World Council itself has also taken very specific positions either indirectly through the CCIA or directly through its Central and Executive Committee. And the World Conference on the issues of Church and Society will certainly also seek to arrive at concrete conclusions on the great social and international issues of our time.

I believe that we have very good reasons to continue along this line. If it is said that the churches should only be concerned with spiritual matters, the answer is surely that concern for the victims of injustice and conflict is a most spiritual matter. If it is argued that the Church must only state general principles, we must say that we have no right to give only counsels of perfection to statesmen and other leaders who are faced with the ambiguities of politics and have so often to choose between various courses each of which may have grave consequences. If we are told that the Church has no competence in this field, we must answer by mobilizing the thought and energy of our ablest Christian laymen who do know the problems concerned. But I believe also that we have not yet worked out a sufficiently clear theology and methodology concerning our witness in these fields. We need more thought on the fundamental issues concerning the presence of the Church in the world. We need more definite criteria as to the choice of issues on which we should speak. We need to clarify in whose behalf each statement is made. The forthcoming World Conference on Church and Society and the consultation in which we plan to discuss the future work of the CCIA are opportunities to arrive at clearer definition. We need on this point the help of theologians, of church administrators, of Christian laymen in different professions. The task is to state what is involved in the Church's office of the watchman who warns the people in the name of the Lord.

107

AFTER THE SECOND VATICAN COUNCIL

At this meeting of our Central Committee we will give careful consideration to the significance of the Second Vatican Council for our own task. Our two permanent observers, who have performed their difficult task with exceptional ability and with a deep sense of their responsibility for the total ecumenical cause, will submit their final reports. I will therefore confine myself to the following general remarks.

Just before the beginning of the Vatican Council we said: *nostra res agitur*—this is also our very real concern. Today we can say this with even deeper meaning. We have followed what happened in the Aula of St. Peter not as mere spectators but as those involved in a crucial event in church history which required our inner participation. We were involved because the existence of our movement was one of the reasons for holding the Vatican Council. We were involved because we are all struggling with the task of renewal in our churches and we could learn so much from the self-examination and rejuvenation which the Vatican Council undertook. We were involved by our grateful assent to conciliar decisions, by our disagreement or disappointment in other matters.

It is inevitable that in relation to a Church Council which has dealt with so many crucial questions there should be different reactions in the other churches. But it seems to me that we must all rejoice in the real awareness which it has shown of the existence of the wider Christian family and that not only through the new language spoken in the *Decree on Ecumenism,* but in a number of other decisions and in the truly fraternal reception given to the observers from other churches.

This means that we are now in a situation in which all churches recognize the simple truth, neglected for centuries, that all Christian churches bear a common responsibility for the total Christian cause.

It will take time to work out the implications of this rediscovery. There is so much in our inherited attitudes, in our structures, in our ecclesiological teaching that holds us back. So we live for the time being in a period with contradictory aspects. The *de facto* developments are ahead of the *de iure* definitions. On the one hand, none of the basic doctrinal issues which have kept us apart has been resolved; and in the matter of the true order of the church, the situation after the Second Vatican Council is not essentially different from that of the First Vatican Council. On the other hand, we have fine fraternal relations such as have found expression in the large meetings in many places during the recent Week of Prayer for Christian Unity. At the same time, unsuspected possibilities of consultation and cooperation have appeared. In most of the fields in which the World Council operates we now find opportunities for fruitful fraternal exchange of convictions and experiences. And we have far more common positions to advocate and to defend than we ever thought possible. A comparative study of WCC statements with the statements of the Vatican Council would reveal a remarkable number of analogies and agreements. This is especially true in the realm of the witness of the Church on the life of the world. We need only think of such subjects as religious liberty, the Christian attitude to the Jewish people, disarmament, the race problem, or the division of the world into rich and poor nations.

In such a situation it has become necessary for the WCC and

the Roman Catholic Church to consider together how the new developments can be so directed that they will serve the best interests of the total ecumenical cause. That is why the Working Group between the WCC and the Roman Catholic Church was set up a year ago. The group will bring its report to this meeting of the Central Committee. It will be for the Central Committee to say whether it approves the recommendations worked out by the group and whether it wants to propose to the authorities of the Roman Catholic Church that the group should continue its work.

Those of us who have been engaged in this work are keenly aware that our task is not to work out a position beyond the positions which have been adopted by the WCC and the Roman Catholic Church, but to find out what in the light of their declared policies we can do together. The governing principles in working out these and all other relationships must be that ecumenism is indivisible. This means that we must constantly be aware of the concerns and convictions of all parts of our own constituency, and also of all Christians who stand outside our fellowship. It means that we must see the task of the WCC as one part of a wide task in which all churches are involved and all have to take their own initiatives. It means that what is being done anywhere to advance the cause of Christian unity is a gift to all the churches.

IN CONCLUSION

At the end of the report which I gave in 1946 to the Geneva meeting of the Provisional Committee of the WCC I said that we were tempted to see its future as a large question mark and to ask whether the Council would still exist some twenty years hence. But I added that such questioning was to commit the sin of looking at the life of the Church as if there were no Holy Spirit. The twenty years have gone. We may say in all humility and gratitude that the Council not only does exist but has been and is being used for the divine action that became manifest at Pentecost. So we may hope that as long as it is needed, it will continue to be an instrument by which the Holy Spirit gathers the scattered children of God for their common mission to the world.

IV.

Unity Among Christians
in the *Decree on Ecumenism*

BY AUGUSTIN CARDINAL BEA

IT HAS OFTEN been said and written that the three sessions of
the Second Vatican Council terminated by awakening "mixed
emotions," by leaving a "conflicting impression," or by having
had a "bitter ending." Far be it from me, as can be seen in all
of my ecumenical statements, to gloss over such problems, to
toss them off as insignificant or to embellish them. True ecumenical thinking requires unwavering honesty which has the
courage to look difficulty straight in the eye. On the other hand,
to think ecumenically in no way means primarily to see only
difficulties or mistakes. Ecumenism stems from love; but love
"does not rejoice at wrong, but rejoices in the right" (1 Cor. 13,
6). One important feature of true ecumenism is, therefore, the
calmly weighed view which above all sees the good and positive
aspects of a given situation. Only in this sense can one also
correctly judge and evaluate that which is insufficient, faulty,
and difficult.

When we ask, in this spirit, what contribution the Second
Vatican Council has made thus far to the unity of Christians, I
feel that on the reader's behalf I must pose the problem con-
cretely as follows: What attitude does the Second Vatican Coun-

cil assume—in particular in its well-known and now definitively promulgated *Decree on Ecumenism*—towards non-Catholics in general and reformed Christians specifically, in order to create a truly fraternal Christian atmosphere? When I say "attitude" I mean critical examination and opinion of non-Catholic Christians, as concerns both the individual and organizations (churches, church communities). This critical evaluation is the basis of the theoretical and practical attitude of the *Decree on Ecumenism* towards the ecumenical movement as such.

The first and fundamental fact is this: One cannot impute the sin of separation to those who at present are born into these communities now separated from the Catholic Church but who are infused with Christ's faith. The Church positively acknowledges that whoever believes in Christ and has been properly baptized or christened shall thereby be vindicated and incorporated into the body of Christ. Therefore, such persons have a right to be honored by the title of Christian, and are properly regarded by the sons of the Catholic Church as brothers in the Lord (No. 3) and shall stand together in certain, though imperfect union with the Catholic Church itself.

Based on this conclusion, the Decree infers that outside the visible boundaries of the Catholic Church, some, and even quite a few of the most significant elements or endowments which together go to build up and give life to the Church itself can exist: the word of God in holy Scripture, the life of grace, the virtues of faith, hope, and love, along with other interior gifts of the Holy Spirit.

The liturgical acts of the Christian religion which are carried out by our separated brethren, each according to the particular version of his respective church or community, are also acknowledged as an appropriate means of access to the community of grace which could undoubtedly bespeak a life of grace. Despite the imperfections inherent in these disunited churches and communities, according to the Catholic point of view, they are not without significance and consequence in God's system of salvation. They use the spirit of Christ as their means towards salvation, the efficacy of which is derived from the bounty of blessings bestowed upon the Catholic Church.

The Council feels that it is the duty of each Catholic person to acknowledge and deeply respect the truly Christian qualities inherent in the churches of all of its separated brethren. It is only right and salutary, proclaims the Decree, to recognize the riches of Christ and the works of the three virtues in the lives of others who are bearing witness to Christ sometimes even to the shedding of the last drop of their blood (No. 4). "Nor should we forget that whatever is wrought by the grace of the Holy Spirit in the hearts of our separated brethren can contribute to our own edification" (No. 4). And this even represents a contribution to the Catholic Church: "Whatever is truly Christian never conflicts with the genuine interests of the faith; indeed, it can always result in a more ample realization of the very mystery of Christ and the Church" (No. 4). These ruptures are, therefore, particularly detrimental and grievous to the Church because they prevent it from effecting the fullness of catholicity which is an intrinsic part of its being in each and every one of its sons who, though joined to it by baptism, are still separated from full communion with the Church.

Honest and complete recognition of that which our non-Catholic brethren possess should not prevent ecumenically-minded Catholics from recognizing just as honestly whatever

114

separates them from one another. The Decree emphasizes this in an extremely clear manner: "Nevertheless, our separated brethren, whether considered as individuals or as Communities and Churches, are not blessed with that unity which Jesus Christ wished to bestow on all those whom He has regenerated and vivified into one body and newness of life—that unity which the Holy Scriptures and the revered tradition of the Church proclaim. For it is through Christ's Catholic Church alone, which is the all-embracing means of salvation, that the fullness of the means of salvation can be obtained" (No. 3). Baptism creates so great a sacramental bond of unity among all Christians who are reborn by means of it, that it is merely a beginning and a point of departure, since, by its very nature, it engenders the attainment of the richness of life in Christ and unity with Christ and in Christ.

Of what does this unity consist? Jesus Christ desires his people to grow in love, strengthened by the Holy Spirit, through the true teachings of the Gospel, through the keeping of the sacraments by the apostles and their followers, the bishops, with St. Peter as their head, and through their accomplishments. He perfects His people's fellowship in unity: "in the confession of one faith, and in the fraternal harmony of the family of God" (No. 2).

It goes without saying that such unity does not mean uniformity. The Council expressly reminds us, in any attempts at safeguarding unity, which is essential, also to allow proper liberty in the various forms of spiritual life and discipline, in the variety of liturgical rites, and even in the theological elaborations of revealed truth. It then adds, in a significant manner: "If the faithful are true to this course of action, they will be giving ever richer expression to the authentic catholicity of the Church, and, at the same time, to her apostolicity" (No. 4).

In expressing itself thus, the Decree does not ignore the many and profound differences in religious doctrine and dogma, but expresses the hope that gradually, by means of a dialogue based on Scripture, the mighty hand of God will bring about the unity which our Saviour holds out to all men (No. 21).

A word is appropriate here concerning the frequently deplored changes made in the *Decree on Ecumenism* which have been responsible, to a considerable extent, for the disharmony with which the third session terminated. One of the primary changes involved ideas on the reading of the Scriptures by our non-Catholic brethren, and on the results of this practice. The difficulty created by this change can only be briefly dealt with in this article. At least this much can be said: it arose for the most part from a misunderstanding. In its present form, the Decree does not in any way disavow (and, as such, would not be able to disavow) the doctrine set forth in the New Testament to the effect that our non-Catholic brethren, just like any baptized person, generally speaking, remain under the guidance of the Holy Spirit, and that this, consequently, holds even more true when they are performing an act as holy as reading the word of God in holy Scripture.

In another place the Council expresses the view that holy Scripture is, indeed, the inspired word of God. Therefore, it is God himself who speaks to man when the Scriptures are read. Thus the often cited version of the corresponding passage in the Decree according to which the disunited brethren seek God in the Holy Scripture "as if He [God] spoke to them in Christ" is simply false. Instead, this sentence should read: "At the invo-

116

cation of the Holy Spirit they [non-Catholics] seek God in holy Scripture as he speaks to them in Christ." Thus this text change does not contain any disavowal of any of the designated truths. Its purpose is merely to emphasize the intention of the text more clearly, and, above all, simply and exclusively to point out the attitude of our non-Catholic brethren in reading Scripture, but not the objective effect of such reading. Evaluation of the objective effect is treated further on where it is stated that in accordance wih Catholic beliefs, an authentic teaching office plays a special role in explaining and proclaiming the written word of God (No. 21).

Sincere emphasis on the differences in belief and on the tremendous difficulties blocking the way towards unity does not prevent the Council from recognizing and evaluating positively the ecumenical movement under way among non-Catholic Christians. This is not only acknowledged repeatedly; it is as if it were instilled and prompted by the Holy Spirit. At the end of the Decree the Council strongly admonishes Catholics to see to it that ". . . the initiatives of the sons of the Catholic Church, joined with those of the separated brethren, go forward without obstructing the ways of divine Providence and without prejudging the future inspiration of the Holy Spirit" (No. 24).

It is unfortunately impossible, within the framework of this article, to deal in detail with the individual aspects of this sort of cooperation in the ecumenical movement. A few remarks will have to suffice. But most important of all is the fact that it has been clearly and ceremoniously stressed that regaining unity is a task for the entire Church, for the faithful as well as for the clergy, each according to his position (No. 5). Modernization of the Church is mentioned as a chief means of accomplishing this.

117

So long as the Church is a man-made institution it will always require revision of its ethics, of its disciplines, and even of the preaching of its doctrine (whereby a clear distinction must be made between manner of preaching and actual dogma).

For the individual Catholic this modernization signifies an inner change, and, as a result thereof, a truly Christian life involving performance of one's duty, self-denial, humility, patient service, brotherly love, all of which is connected with this love: reciprocal forgiveness, respect, and brotherly assistance.

In particular, however, prayer is recommended. It is permissible and even desirable for Catholics to sit together in prayer with their separated brethren on special occasions such as during a prayer for unity or at an ecumenical gathering. "Such prayers in common are certainly a very effective means of petitioning for the grace of unity, and they are a genuine expression of the ties which even now bind Catholics to their separated brethren" (No. 8).

The Decree urgently and repeatedly recommends theological discussion between well-instructed experts from the various churches or communities in which ". . . each explains the teaching of his Communion in greater depth and brings out clearly its distinctive features. Through such dialogue, everyone gains a truer knowledge and more just appreciation of the teaching and religious life of both Communions" (No. 4).

Fraternal cooperation is advocated just as avidly, the purpose of which is to ". . . contribute to a just appreciation of the dignity of the human person, the promotion of the blessings of peace, the application of gospel principles to social life, and the advancement of the arts and sciences in a Christian spirit. Christians should also work together in the use of every possible

118

means to relieve the afflictions of our times, such as famine and natural disasters, illiteracy and poverty, lack of housing, and the unequal distribution of wealth." ". . . [A]ll men without exception" are summoned to united effort in such tasks. "Those who believe in God have a stronger summons, but the strongest claims are laid on Christians, since they have been sealed with the name of Christ. Cooperation among all Christians vividly expresses that bond which already unites them, and it sets in clearer relief the features of Christ the Servant" (No. 12).

The *Decree on Ecumenism,* calmly and objectively examined, is a very significant and meaningful offshoot of the third Council session. The few incidents which occurred and which caused many a disappointment during the last few days of the Council do not alter this fact. These incidents should in no way lead one seriously to question the fostering of ecumenical attitudes. He who has experienced such events at close range and is familiar with all related aspects of them also knows that under the prevailing conditions, things essentially could not have gone much differently than the way they went. This explanation leaves a great deal to be desired, but the time available does not allow further elaboration. In any case we should look forward to the fourth Council session with complete and utter confidence.

Even before the Council, Professor K. Skydsgaard, director of the Lutheran Institute for Ecumenical Research in Copenhagen, who took part in all three Council sessions as an official observer of the Lutheran World Federation, wrote as follows: "What happens in the Roman Catholic Church cannot be unimportant to Protestants. . . . The Council's objectives pose an unavoidable problem for us" (*The Council and the Gospel*). If this already applied to the Council's objectives, it applies even more to the

Council's outcome. It is quite evident how much the Holy Spirit is at work here. If this is the case, then what happened at the Council represents a powerful appeal to all Christians. The work of the Spirit of God in the ecumenical movement, as expressly set forth in the *Decree on Ecumenism,* has stirred the Catholic Church to take up its ecumenical burden and to give all Catholics guidance and instruction by means of lengthy and exhaustive consultations and conferences.

In this way the same Spirit of God, to which the drawing up of this Decree in the Council bears witness, serve as a new appeal to all Christians to seek zealously, persistently, and in fraternal harmony, the unity of God's Church which He desires, to pray for it, to struggle for it, and to suffer for it in the same way as did Pope John XXIII upon heralding the Council.

V.

Characterization of the Present Situation

BY AUGUSTIN CARDINAL BEA

1. Address at the Ecumenical Center in Geneva. February 18, 1966

Dear Brothers in Christ!

I do not feel that any name I might use to greet you would be more appropriate at this time, which we may certainly call awe-inspiring, and which represents a magnificent gift from the God of the Church to us all. In the same way I have repeatedly had the pleasure of welcoming so many churches and world federations (and, among them, observers from the World Council of Churches as well) to the Council since October, 1962. For the name "Brothers in Christ" summarizes the deepest meaning of that which is common to us all as a consequence of the holy baptism on which our roots and foundations in love, and therefore in Christ, are based. The name "Brothers in Christ" also summarizes the spirit in which we must meet one another and wish to meet one another, whatever faith or creed we might belong to. Finally, this name expresses our goal: We want to be brothers in Christ to the fullest extent, and we therefore want to be wholly one in the manner in which He wants us to be one.

What is the first thought we must express as a sign of greeting if not our joyful thanks to God, giver of all good things, for granting us this hour, this meeting itself and all that it means and promises? In August, 1962, I was in London and was able to pay a visit to Dr. Michael Ramsey, the Archbishop of Canterbury and Primate of all of England. The purpose of my trip was to return the visit paid by his predecessor, Lord Fisher, to Pope John XXIII in December, 1960. He came forward to meet me on the steps, embraced me, and said: "Your Eminence, this is a historical event. Since the time of Cardinal Pole, no cardinal of the Roman Church has set foot in this palace!"

Similarly, although for other reasons, our meeting today may also be viewed as a historical one. We know that this has not been the case for many centuries. Here is not the place to outline the history of these past centuries or to enter into details. It shall suffice to state what we all know, namely that things were entirely different throughout many centuries. After Pope John XXIII founded the Secretariat for Promoting Christian Unity, the establishment of contacts began, such as, primarily, our sending official observers to the Third General Assembly of the World Council of Churches in New Delhi, and your sending observers to the Vatican Council, not to mention the various contacts of a more private and confidential nature.

But our meeting today is of special importance, and its sense is enhanced by virtue of the concrete historical context in which it takes place. This, in essence, is a meeting which has been long in preparation; I am not thinking of this so much from the technical point of view as from the point of view of psychological preparation, that is, as concerns the series of contacts established and developed gradually over the past five years, since the founding of the Secretariat for Promoting Christian Unity, with many of the churches who are members of the World Council as well as with their main headquarters here in Geneva. The most meaningful and far-reaching of these contacts were the long-lasting ones occurring during the three sessions of the Second Vatican Council. Furthermore, this is a meeting which is strongly influenced by the *Decree on Ecumenism* which was approved and promulgated in November of last year with only 11 out of 2,000 Council Fathers dissenting. This vote is an indication of the progressively more serious ecumenical atmosphere which the Council meeting brought about. This atmosphere also exerted a profound influence on many members of the Catholic episcopate who, for various reasons, had never before been confronted in their own actual experience with the problem of Christianity's schism and with ecumenical attitudes. The Council allowed them to look at this schism in terms of its actual form, to reflect deeply on it, to undertake making the first contacts with non-Catholic brethren, and thus gradually to put themselves in an ecumenical frame of mind. The result of this was that even before the *Decree on Ecumenism* was set down on paper, its contents had already constituted a true and actual experience on the part of the majority of those in the Catholic episcopate throughout the world. They therefore experienced a highly positive manner of looking upon their non-Catholic brethren and the relationship of the latter to the Catholic Church, which is expressed in the Decree. They were also able to experience that distinctly loyal and at the same time very positive concept of the goal to be achieved, that is, the unity of the Church, in its relationship to legitimate freedom and diversity, as these, too, are expressed in the Decree. Finally, they considered at length the long-range plan for future ecumenical work set forth in the

Decree on Ecumenism. So, one could say that in the Decree, the actual personal experience of the Council Fathers was merely set down on paper; therefore, the Decree is not merely a series of beautiful words, its text is much more an expression of the Catholic Church's sincere and strong desire, which, for its part, is the best guarantee that the Decree will be put into action.

Viewed in the concrete context of a Council Decree which is based on the experience of the Catholic episcopate itself, this meeting appears also as a symbol of fruitful prospects for further progress. Similarly, just as contacts exist within the framework of the World Council of Churches, on the one hand among various churches who are members of the World Council, and on the other hand among the member churches and the World Council itself, the Secretariat for Promoting Christian Unity (and through this Secretariat the Holy See itself) has made contacts and wishes to develop them either by direct contacts with the individual churches and federations in the Eastern as well as in the Western world, or else by means of contacts with the World Council of Churches itself. In this sense we welcome with joy the unanimous decision taken by the Third Panortho-dox Conference in November of last year when, despite the impossibilities it foresaw, it nevertheless immediately began a theological dialogue with the Catholic Church on behalf of the entire Orthodox Church, and even recommended to all churches that each of them make and develop its own direct contacts with the Catholic Church. The Holy See, in the same manner, accepts with joy and welcomes unreservedly (and I am especially pleased that I may officially make the announcement on this occasion) the proposal made last month by the Executive Committe of the World Council of Churches in Enugu to the effect that a mixed

124

committee be set up, to be composed of eight representatives from the World Council of Churches and six from the Catholic Church, and the purpose of which will be to research together the possibility of dialogue and concerted effort between the World Council of Churches and the Catholic Church. As we already know, the task of this committee will not be to reach decisions of any type whatsoever, but rather simply to explore the principles and methods on which possible future dialogue and collaboration might be based and realized. The results of this committee's work will then be submitted to the responsible parties on each side for further examination and for drafting of the corresponding decisions. I have no doubt that this step, which corresponds so appropriately to the text and spirit of the Council Decree, will bring good results, be they in the area of mutual cooperation in solving the major and urgent problems of our time, or in the area of dialogue, in the true sense of this word.

What I have just set forth concerning the historical significance of our meeting today, and the fruits it will assuredly bear, does not at all mean that we ignore the numerous obstacles and difficulties which lie in our way. We have seen examples of this at the conclusion of the third Council session, and they were by no means the last. Everything depends on our not becoming discouraged, and in our meeting these difficulties with courage and with the faith that moves mountains. These difficulties, whatever type they may be, are no reason why brothers should turn away from one another in distrust. On the contrary, our brotherly love and our love of unity should give us the courage to discuss everything openly, even the most difficult problems. This also applies to discussion of the most delicate questions, those pertaining to doctrine. We all share a common basis for such discussions: the word of God in holy Scripture, the concrete expression of which is accounted for in the thoughts and ideas of the Fathers of the Eastern and Western worlds. Apropos of this, Dr. Ramsey, the Archbishop of Canterbury, said in New Delhi, "One finds an interest among Roman Catholics, Lutherans, Orthodox, Calvinists, and Anglicans in the Bible, in the Church Fathers, and in liturgy which changes the conditions of thought and the representation of doctrine, and creates new bases for discussion and unification." We therefore want to examine our doctrine in the light of our complete trust in the truth of Christ, and also in the light of love, with all the mutual respect and esteem, understanding and good will that this implies. In this way, confidence in the truth will not be cause for distrust any more than it will be cause for new separations. The mercy of Christ will be with us in such sincere efforts. This mercy is powerful enough to lead us to each and every truth, in accordance with the Lord's promise; it will help us forever to discover anew and wholly to protect the treasure of truth which Christ entrusted to the Church He founded.

Thus, let us not look upon each other with distrust or with a critical mind, but rather in the spirit of emulation in love and good works (Heb. 10, 24). The *Decree on Ecumenism* reminds us that those values which are really Christian never stand in contrast to the true values of faith; to the contrary, these can help translate into reality the secret of Christ and the Church (No. 4). This Decree similarly explains that the very consideration of that which the ecumenical movement has put into practice towards its non-Catholic brethren has proved to be a stimulus and invitation for the Council to take up the ecumenical problem itself in order to transmit to all Catholics the information and instructions necessary for the movement. In accordance with the wish Pope John expressed upon announcing the Council, we must therefore hope that those events which the Holy Spirit brought about at the Council and by means of the Council will constitute an invitation to our non-Catholic brethren to seek even more zealously the unity which Christ invoked and desired. Even if realization of this unity is not only difficult for us but actually exceeds our human powers and abilities, as is emphasized in the *Decree on Ecumenism,* we must nevertheless place our entire trust in Christ's prayer for the Church, on the Father's love for us, and on the power of the Holy Spirit. "And hope does not disappoint us, because God's love has been poured into our hearts through the Holy Spirit which is given to us" (Rom. 5, 5; No. 24).

2. The Church in New Directions.
Interview with a Member of the Protestant Press Service

Question: A representative of the World Council recently stated in Rome that acceptance of the *Decree on Ecumenism* would signify "the beginning of the dialogue on the dialogue." From that date on, this sentence certainly seems to infer, the disunited churches would discuss the possible putting into action of their official dialogue. Are you, too, of this opinion, and what suggestions could you make concerning this new stage in ecumenical activity?

Answer: I am basically in agreement with this view. In this connection, it must indeed be noted that we do not find ourselves at the very beginning, for dialogue of a somewhat different nature has already taken place in various countries.

As far as suggestions are concerned, we would do better not to consider this aspect at the present time. The reason is quite simple. The position and attitude of church leaders and communities are so different in the various countries and even within the various churches in these various countries that generalized suggestions cannot be made. It would be more practical first to explore the territory in question by means of preliminary talks held among the responsible parties themselves, and then to work out suggestions together on the basis of these preliminary steps. After all, even though this method might take longer, it is still the best indication of our mutual trust in Christ insofar as we would not be submitting carefully premeditated proposals, as one does in politics; these proposals would be achieved through the hard work of discussions based on confidence. And this work would be facilitated by the fact that the main tenets of our attitude towards ecumenical endeavor and dialogue have been set down in detail by the Council's *Decree on Ecumenism*.

Perhaps one last word would be appropriate. It has become a matter of course that theological discussions, important as they may be, are no longer considered the sole means of promoting unity. In addition to this possibility there is a whole series of other methods by which the ecumenical attitude may be demonstrated and expressed. We have only to think of prayer, of mutual respect and love, of the true Christian life, of cooperation, and of concerted action in various practical areas. These methods are of no less importance, and also entail valuable and often indispensable preparation of a more remote nature, for the creation of the only appropriate atmosphere for discussion, which is an atmosphere of mutual trust, understanding, and love.

Question: The non-Catholic asks himself what spiritual reality actually lies behind the Council's vote on the *Decree on Ecumenism*. In view of the fact that this text contains an abundance of ideas and definitions which would have been completely unthinkable ten years ago, especially here in Rome, we would like to ask the following question: Has so much really changed in these past few years or has the Council anticipated a future reality by means of this text?

Answer: Behind the *Decree on Ecumenism* the spiritual-supernatural reality created by the Council's winding up of activity does exist. We are perhaps not yet giving due consideration to the tremendous impact this event elicited in the Church among both Catholic and non-Catholic Christians. A double encounter took place at the Council, the meeting of all the Catholic bishops of the whole world with each other, and their meeting with the representatives of so many non-Catholic churches and world federations of churches. The effect of the latter can hardly be underestimated and has not been sufficiently appreciated to date in terms of its magnitude and enormous consequences. Marc Boegner, the well-known French ecumenical pastor, exposed these consequences movingly in a lecture delivered in Rome. I myself am able to state publicly that the non-Catholic observer delegates made a decisive contribution to the *Decree on Ecumenism*. Of course they did not prepare this Decree and did not participate directly in the Council debates and voting. But their presence at the Council and their participation in the form of prayer, study, and all types of contacts and

129

suggestions allowed the Council Fathers to experience the ecumenical problem profoundly and from all points of view. In this way we all became progressively more aware of the unity in Christ existing among us, equally aware of the many things which separate us, and thereby aware of the many difficulties implied in our ecumenical work. Perhaps, vice versa, similar reflection on the effects of the Council on non-Catholic Christians and their churches could be initiated. It shall suffice merely to hint at this here. The *Decree on Ecumenism* itself is a concrete written embodiment of all these experiences which, in themselves, in my opinion, will prove to be much more important and more fruitful than the Decree itself, as is, of course, unavoidably necessary.

You can see from the foregoing that profound changes have actually come about in the Church in these last few years; we shall not be able to account for them until a certain amount of time has elapsed. Thus far the experience of all Christians at the Council may be compared to the small mustard seed in the Gospel which unfolds in order to show itself in its full meaning and size.

You have indeed understood that the *Decree on Ecumenism also* represents something to look forward to. One could perhaps express this more precisely as a "long-range plan." Why not? If it is the job of every intelligent lawmaker to anticipate later developments and make provisions for them, then one must expect the same thing of a lawmaking body such as the Church. The plan becomes gradually simpler as the entire work of the Council progresses under the powerful holy influence of the Church's guiding light, the Spirit of Christ, which is the most essential one at the Council. The enormous changes just described evolved due to the presence of this spirit. Under its guidance the Council also endeavored to foresee further projects and give them a definite direction.

Question: The language, and in part the contents, too, of the *Decree on Ecumenism* and a few other Council texts contradict the sentences of condemnation of the Council of Trent and of several papal encyclicals. Can we expect these sentences of condemnation to be repealed, and how could this be done?

Answer: In order to give your readers a clear idea of the meaning of your last question, I must first pose a question in return. The Protestant church has been contributing to the ecumenical movement for decades and, in so doing, has made its ecumenical attitude known. In this connection, was it ever considered to remove from the confessions of faith the judgments of condemnation and those sentences which designate the pope as "anti-Christ"? As you know, even today the *damnamus* is repeated along with the pledge to heed the confessions of faith, at almost all ordinations of ministers.

But let us penetrate into the problem itself. I do not see how one can speak about an actual contradiction existing between the sentences of condemnation promulgated by the Council of Trent and the contents of the *Decree on Ecumenism.* One should certainly call to mind the corresponding passage in Pope John XXIII's opening address to the Council. He says, "The Church has always opposed these errors. Frequently she has condemned them with the greatest severity. Today, however, the Spouse of Christ prefers to use the medicine of mercy rather than of severity. She considers that she meets the needs of the present day more by demonstrating the validity of her teaching than by condemnation. There is, to be sure, no lack of fallacious teachings, opinions, and dangerous concepts that must be guarded against and put to flight."

In saying this, the pope is not denouncing the Church's qualifications as far as its former conduct throughout the centuries is concerned. But he is saying that the Church *today* considers other conduct more practical. What is *always* of direct concern to the Church is absolute faith in Christ and in the religious doctrine He entrusted to her. She values this gift so highly that no price or effort is too great to preserve it. It is precisely this view of the discomfort caused by the denominational separation of Christians today which impressively reveals to us this attitude of the Church and its unavoidable necessity. This noble goal, the purity and unity of faith, should have served as a corresponding method of action to the thinking in terms of anathemas which took place in times gone by. Its primary meaning and purpose was to make the Church's binding doctrines unequivocally and effectively clear, and to discourage Church members from abandoning them. To the extent that this concerns elucidation of doctrine and condemnation of mutually committed errors, there is no doubt whatever that the sentences of condemnation from the Council of Trent must remain in existence in the future. I myself have repeatedly explained in my lectures (and I know that this explanation has been accepted sincerely by truly ecumenically-minded non-Catholic Christians) that we can promise no one a retraction or mitigation of the Tridentine Council's dogmatic decisions on doctrine by the Second Vatican Council, or that we shall require of non-Catholic Christians mere acknowledgment of so-called "important dogmas." For a "dogma" is precisely a truth which belongs essentially to the treasure of religious teachings entrusted to the Church. To the extent that these sentences of condemnation are directed towards the "weak," to use the familiar expression of St. Paul (see Rom. 14, 1), that is, to protect the less experienced and less enlightened from any dangers which might threaten the purity of their faith, they could, of course, not be rejected in essence unless we reject that which St. Paul and the Lord himself rejected. Did not Christ the Lord denounce with the harshest of words those who offended the "little ones" and who thereby exposed them to eternal corruption (see Matt. 18, 6 and Lk. 17, 2). And did not Paul deliver Hymanaeus and Alexander to Satan (see 1 Tim. 1, 20), no matter how biblical interpreters might wish to explain this controversial utterance?

This, and this alone, is what the Church's sentences of condemnation mean; they do not mean that during a man's lifetime the Church will sit in judgment on his salvation and condemn him to hell. On the contrary, just as St. Paul's "delivery to Satan" is ultimately intended "for the destruction of the flesh, that his spirit may be saved in the day of the Lord Jesus" (1 Cor. 5, 5), so it is with the Church; she, too, in addition to protecting the weak from having their faith offended, performs the deed of converting those who offend. Even though the Church does not choose to retract the sentences of condemnation at this time, she desires even less to sit in judgment on non-Catholic Christians who observe any of the condemned doctrines. She knows (and expresses this conviction in the *Decree on Ecumenism*) that they have been born and bred into their creeds and consider their confession, in all good faith, as an expression of their loyalty towards Christ. Thus, even though the Church's judgment on the errors contradicting her doctrines shall un-

133

questionably continue to remain in existence, it still does not contain any condemnation of individuals. This applies to the acknowledgment of good faith, and thereby to the reverence and love expressed in the *Decree on Ecumenism*. This should explain the significance of the Church's sentences of condemnation in the light of the Scripture and of Pope John XXIII's solemn declaration. It should also be an understood fact that this declaration, from the point of view of severity as well as of benevolence, corresponds to holy Scripture and therefore to the true educational wisdom of the Church.

Question: It has often been said that future relationships between the various faiths will depend largely on how the questions of religious liberty, proselytism, and mixed marriage are answered. What has already been seen at the Council, and what could still be done to eliminate these obstacles to the dialogue?

Answer: As far as religious liberty is concerned, you are aware of the fact that the document on this subject (which allows for minor and fundamentally insignificant changes, but which established the basic text) was accepted by a vast majority of bishops. Nevertheless, we must bear in mind that it is precisely this aggressive proselytism of many non-Catholic sects in South America which has caused so much trouble to the Catholic bishops from the respective countries in carrying out their responsibility towards their followers, and which has rendered due appreciation of the *Declaration on Religious Freedom* rather difficult. The text of this Declaration is well-known along general lines, and has been widely acclaimed by several non-Catholic Church leaders, as the press reported at that time.

134

As far as the question of mixed marriage is concerned, I must mention the fact that this problem varies greatly according to the different countries and continents. We must therefore guard against judging the entire issue on the basis of one single country. For just this reason the Council was unable to provide a generally accepted solution to the problem. But the corresponding Document, in its present form, strongly stresses the ecumenical side of the problem, and furnishes general guidelines for appropriate handling of the conditions set forth, to the extent that these remain in existence. This is all that the Council, which must have the entire Church and the entire world in mind, can do in view of the diversity of the problem. At any rate we must have a clear concept of the meaning of marriage from a Christian viewpoint. For it goes without saying that all pertinent measures must be carefully considered and dealt with in the light of Christian doctrine on the nature and requirements of marriage.

Question: How will the future work envisaged by the Secretariat for Promoting Christian Unity which you head be fashioned? Will it be adjusted to ideas brought up at the Council? Will it be called upon during the post-counciliar period to draw legal and practical conclusions from Council decisions and arrive at a uniform interpretation and explanation thereof? What importance do you attribute to this postconciliar period?

Answer: The Secretariat intends to deal with its own tasks after the Council as it did before and during the Council. Its responsibility is not to draw legal and practical conclusions from decisions taken by the Council. One of its first jobs will be to work out the ecumenical "Directorate" which has been announced on various occasions, and in which more detailed guidelines and principles for Catholic ecumenical work can be formulated without creating a situation of undue uniformity and centralization. This also involves the establishment of contacts among various ecumenical enterprises and undertakings on the Catholic side so that Catholics can come to know each other and exchange experiences. Parallel with this, we must cultivate and broaden the contacts with non-Catholic churches or their world federations which were established during the pre-conciliar period and during the Council itself for the purpose of making plans for further cooperation, as stated above, and, as far as possible, for the purpose of promoting and organizing discussions on theology.

As far as post-conciliar work is concerned, it is obvious that the Secretariat, too, will have its say in the regulations set forth in the Council Decrees, as well as in preparations or actual holding of the Council meetings, to the extent that ecumenical interests come into question.

But the more important matter is for the Secretariat not to stand alone in safeguarding ecumenical interests even in this phase of development. The vote on the *Decree on Ecumenism* clearly indicated that the ecumenical spirit has become the common property of the Council Fathers. But even more than the *Decree on Ecumenism* itself, this attitude on the part of the bishops who are going to become involved in the various post-conciliar commissions is the best guarantee that ecumenical problems will be duly borne in mind during post-conciliar work as well.

Question: Based on the current status of Council negotiations do you foresee the possibility of new discussions between separated Christians on the dogmatic issues which are the cause of their separation? From this point of view, how do you judge the Council's interpretation of Scripture and tradition with regard to Mary, the controversial mediatrix concept, and the Church office, namely, the primacy?

Answer: The possibilities are assuredly vast. To a considerable extent, they have been created by the Council itself. In the lectures I delivered before the Council convened, I repeatedly indicated that we must not only consider anew problems dealing with differences in doctrine, due account being given to the present state of affairs. Instead, we must seek principles which give due account to the thinking of our interlocutor, and which are easier for him to comprehend. These principles may be obtained, most preferably, by ardent study of holy Scripture (in particular, biblical theology) and of the older traditions. This has already been stated at the Council to a great extent. Moreover, we Catholics, during the Council, have had the opportunity to become more intensively enlightened as to the present-day ideas of non-Catholic churches as a result of the contacts established with the observer delegates. Vice versa, these very same non-Catholic churches have certainly also had the opportunity to acquire first-hand information on the Catholic Church and its teachings by virtue of their observer delegates' participation in the Council. All of these factors have resulted in the creation of entirely new and promising bases for fruitful dialogue.

Concerning the individual subjects you mentioned, it does not seem appropriate to comment on these now. Precisely these points, and a few others as well, must be made the subjects of theological discussions. We must have the courage to examine them trustingly and in a spirit of brotherhood, in the spirit expressed last year at the Montreal Conference on "Faith and Order," that is, in a spirit of unshakable love of the truth and obedience to faith.

I would like to conclude this discussion by expressing my thanks to the Protestant Press Service for giving me this precious opportunity to express a few words to so many Protestant Christians. May I say just one more thing. It has often been stressed by the non-Catholic side, as well, that the Council represents a blessing of our Lord Jesus Christ or the Church, and thereby, for all those who are united with him through the bond of faith and baptism. But a blessing is a "visitation" of the Lord, and on it is based the Lord's admonition not to misjudge the time of the visitation (see Luke 19, 44). The blessed visitation places us all before our increased responsibility towards Christ, the Church, and all of humanity.

3. Orthodoxy and the Catholic Church. Interview with a Greek Journalist

Question: Are the difficulties created by reunification of the Church more practical or more dogmatic in nature?

Answer: I must clearly limit myself here to that which concerns the Catholic and Orthodox churches. The obstacles standing in the way of reunification of the entire religious community are many and varied. Some lie on the level of creed, that is, of the expression of faith, rather than necessarily on the level of faith itself. Others are more practical in nature. It is easy to ascertain the presence of these obstacles, but difficult to pass judgment on their actual importance, for they are inseparable from obstacles of a psychological nature which appear to be the most significant ones by far. And the latter, in fact, precede the others. One could say that they gradually created the others. Varying mentalities which should have complemented each other slowly became estranged from one another. We understood nothing more than this. We ceased feeling we were brothers and ceased treating each other as brothers. We allowed our love to grow cool. We became hardened in our opposition towards one another. We emphasized and magnified the differences between us. We withdrew into our own little worlds. We wanted to justify an actual schism on the Church level which was exclusively or almost exclusively caused by non-theological factors. This attitude formed Christian thinking on both sides for centuries. And now we must reëstablish what the centuries have destroyed.

Question: How would you evaluate these difficulties? Have they perhaps been exaggerated? Can they be overcome purely and simply through an attempt at good will?

Answer: I have just said that the psychological factor greatly contributed towards creating, hardening, and frequently exaggerating these difficulties. However, they do exist today, and we must find a way to overcome them. In this case I would like to call to mind a passage from your liturgy. Before the recitation of the creed, the celebrant turns to the Christian congregation and says, "Let us have love for one another, that we may with one mind confess the Father, the Son, and the Holy

Spirit, the consubstantial and undivided Trinity." This means that the deep bond between confession of faith and brotherly union in love does exist. We saw how, after this brotherly union in love was destroyed, union through creed also degenerated. Creed is an act of Church life, and consequently an expression of this life. Creed is not the result of a discussion between theologians. It occasionally makes use of such discussions for the purpose of arriving at greater precision. But reëstablishment of unity of creed should never be viewed as a result of a compromise based on discussion between experts. This is a question involving infinitely more. If you see this effort as a gesture of good will towards reëstablishing brotherly union in love to an increasingly greater extent through utter mutual trust and respect, then we can say without hesitation that this effort is the necessary point of departure. It is therefore also the irreplaceable basis and stimulating climate for gradual development of mutual understanding, under the guidance of the Holy Spirit, for which every Christian, Catholic or Orthodox, must strive in order to comprehend his own teachings and those of his brothers. You ask me how I might evaluate the difficulties which exist between us. Chief among them is perhaps the function of the bishop of Rome within the universal Church. There are other problems revolving around the doctrine of the holy Virgin. There is the notable question of the *filioque,* but this seems to me to be more a result of mutual misunderstanding than anything else. However, we must make the distinction between dogma, which is the rule of faith and which must of necessity be controlled by unity, and theology, which is the effort of pious intellect to penetrate, explain, and expound upon dogma. A certain diversity on the theological level is legitimate and salutary. This is expressly stated in No. 17 of the *Decree on Ecumenism* which was approved almost unanimously during the third session of the Vatican Council. "In the investigation of revealed truth, East and West have used different methods and approaches in understanding and proclaiming divine things. It is hardly surprising, then, if sometimes one tradition has come nearer than the other to an apt appreciation of certain aspects of a revealed mystery, or has expressed them in a clearer manner. As a result, these various theological formulations are often to be considered as complementary rather than conflicting." The same thought is set forth in No. 4 of the Decree: "While preserving unity in essentials, let all members of the Church, according to the office entrusted to each, preserve a proper freedom in the various forms of spiritual life and discipline, in the variety of liturgical rites, and even in the theological elaborations of revealed truth." No. 23 of the *Dogmatic Constitution on the Church* expresses this idea no less clearly: "By divine Providence it has come about that various churches established in diverse places by the apostles and their successors have in the course of time coalesced into several groups, organically united, which, preserving the unity of faith and the unique divine constitution of the universal Church, enjoy their own discipline, their own liturgical usage, and their own theological and spiritual heritage. . . . This variety of local churches with one common aspiration is particularly splendid evidence of the catholicity of the undivided Church."

You can therefore see that these efforts to reëstablish brotherly union in love are desired by every church. Each must seek to renew and deepen its own traditions. Such work is inseparable from any other effort towards greater faith in Christ, the

Lord of the Church, through prayer or conversion of the heart. I already explained, when I cited your liturgy, that we shall attain unity of creed only if we love one another. And we should not forget that we can truly love one another only if we offer a greater love to Christ and maintain a greater loyalty to Christ throughout our entire Christian lives.

Question: Can this whole issue be seen more as a problem of unification than one of unity of the churches, and what is the precise importance attributed to each of these expressions?

Answer: The very effort of approaching one another and resuming the habit of living together on the various levels of church life, a certain cooperation in the areas of social endeavor, education, and the spiritual charge of a common witness towards non-Christians can bring about and develop such unity. But this unity of action must be the mark of and means by which more profound unification and union in the Holy Spirit may be allowed to grow.

This entire movement towards rapprochement of the Catholic and Orthodox churches is based on reacquiring awareness of the true though imperfect union which already exists and which derives from the profound sense of identity of both churches above and beyond their differences, which, as I have already said, are real ones. This profound sense of identity is firstly that of the sacramental structure of both churches. We have the same sacraments and accept them, on both sides, as being valid. We have the same baptism, and, as Pope Paul VI said on various occasions, we have "the same priesthood which offers the sacrifice of the Lord of the Church." This is the reality which causes both of us to regard ourselves truly as

142

churches in the theological sense of the word. The Fathers of the Vatican Council expressed the same idea clearly and emphatically in No. 5 of the *Decree on Ecumenism*.

Reacquisition of the awareness of this reality must bring both sides to act accordingly. This reality must be translated into deeds, and must penetrate life itself. For example, when Pope Paul VI, "with gladness of heart," returned the precious head of St. Andrew to the church of Patras, he clearly showed, through this act, that he acknowledged the church of Patras as a church, and its bishop as his brother in the bishopric, even though the former did not yet live in complete union with him. Acts such as these express this profound sense of identity, and simultaneously allow it to flourish. They are based on a sense of fellowship which already exists, and, in turn, they allow this fellowship to flourish. The same applies to reciprocal visits paid by the heads of churches, to the exchange of correspondence on the occasion of important holidays, and the like. These are all forms of announcing and practicing a certain state of unity, and all this paves the way towards perfect fellowship while the return of complete union is awaited.

Question: Under what general conditions can such unification or unity of the churches be realized, and what methods must be used in such endeavors to achieve either unification or unity?

Answer: This question resembles the previous one to a considerable extent. I think I have already replied to the second part of your question. As far as the first part is concerned, I must specify the fact that the reëstablishment of complete sacramental and legitimate union between the Catholic and Orthodox churches would in no way signify absorption of one part of Christianity by the other, or subjection of one part of Christianity to the other. Actually, agreement as to the function of the pope in the Church as successor to St. Peter would not at all signify subjection of the Christian East to western Christianity. It would merely imply acknowledgement of a focal point for the community, which is necessary to the entire Church, and a supreme authority within this Church, a focal point and authority which was desired by Christ himself and which is just as necessary to the East as it is to the West. This is therefore not a question of absorption by or subjection to Western Christianity. Instead, it concerns reëstablishment of the "symphony of the holy Church of God" in the manner Christ desired. This is a question of harmony in which legitimately different and diverse churches declare themselves in basic agreement with the fundamental necessity granted to us and desired by Christ. This, therefore, is a question of articulating through love in such manner that we enrich one another by our differences in order to recognize more clearly the true value of the various aspects of Christ's unfathomable riches. No. 16 of the *Decree on Ecumenism* is very clear on this subject: "Far from being an obstacle to the Church's unity, such diversity of customs and observances only adds to her comeliness, and contributes greatly to carrying out her mission, as has already been recalled. To remove any shadow of a doubt, then, this sacred Synod solemnly declares that the Churches of the East, while keeping in mind the necessary unity of the whole Church, have the power to govern themselves according to their own disciplines . . ." When the Church says "power" here, she means "right" and "obligation" at the same time. This is a question of recognizing the canonical autonomy of the eastern churches, within the framework of the discipline instituted by Christ, of course.

Question: How do you view the problem of the united Church within the framework of an effort directed towards reëstablishing unification or unity of the churches?

Answer: As far as the origins and legitimacy of the churches are concerned, this is basically a question of freedom, the freedom of the sons of God. When an individual or a community is driven by its conscience, and desires to associate itself in full fellowship with the Catholic Church, in the belief that this signifies obedience to the Holy Spirit, then the Catholic Church cannot oppose such an individual group, and is of the opinion that it does not have the right to require these individuals or communities to deny their past, their history, their culture, and their rightful religious traditions in order to be assimilated into such a fellowship. The Catholic Church does not wish to latinize all peoples, and believes that variety within unity actually constitutes the catholicity of the Church. The Vatican Council emphasizes and will continue to emphasize the fact that all nations and cultures have the same rights to the Church of Christ. If such a view has not always been respected in the past, this is due to the human weaknesses which fashion the Church, while the basic principles are clear. That is why there are a variety of rites in the Catholic Church which have their own external form and their own tradition. Freedom is the point in question here. It is absurd to see in it a neglect on the part of the Orthodox church or a means of proselytism. Its actual existence is based on a dictate of conscience on the part of a few individuals or communities, and such dictates of a

145

Christian conscience are always worthy of esteem. If, by the grace of God, the perfect union which existed between the Catholic Church and the Orthodox churches is reëstablished, then the united churches would dissappear, by virtue of this very fact.

Question: Are the methods used thus far considered successful ones, and to what extent could they serve as prototypes for further endeavor?

Answer: Up to now we have made the effort to begin our dialogue of love, and I feel that I have expressed the full meaning and depth of this dialogue of love in my reply to your second question. One could say that it has already borne fruits of encouragement. The change in atmosphere in relations between the Roman Catholic Church and the Orthodox church in the last few years is obvious. This does not mean that all distrust and suspicion has disappeared. But a new spirit of love reigns, and this spirit must continue to inspire relations between Catholics and Orthodox. In this sense we can say that the methods used to date may be used as prototypes for future endeavors. But we cannot content ourselves with merely imitating this prototype. Love must be bent creatively and attentively on finding means of expression corresponding to the prevailing conditions and to the individuals in question. As I already stated in connection with the third question, we must reshape our vocation and cooperation in the areas of social work, education, and spiritual guidance in jointly bearing witness towards the rest of the world. We are now merely at the beginning of our concerted endeavors after so many centuries of separation. We must allow the inspiration of the Holy Spirit to continue

146

leading us along our way so that we may follow the course we have just begun to follow.

Question: Do the current tendencies towards unity and cooperation between the churches imply significant changes within the pale of these churches (infallibility, supremacy of the pope, etc.)?

Answer: Such a rapprochement can come about only through trust in Christ, and neither one of the churches has the right to betray its faith. I have stated above that reëstablishment of unity of creed ought never to be the result of a compromise. The Church is not a human society which can alter its laws in accordance with the prevailing conditions. It is bound to Christ, its brother, and subject to the spirit with which Christ imbued it.

But there is one prerequisite for deepening my Church's faith and traditions, for further penetration into ultimately revealed truth, in order to perceive its essence and all of its demands more clearly. We must also know how to distinguish between those elements which are permanent, necessary, and therefore important, and those which are relative and contingent, and which, good as they might be, do not make the same demands on all people, and can therefore vary, as I have already explained. The Catholic Church has begun to make this effort. Every church must make it. Moreover, many facets of it can be carried out in cooperation. All too often we regard such contacts and dialogue as if they constituted a debate on controversial issues. But this is only one aspect of the story. There is another aspect, too, a more fruitful one: we must join forces,

147

examine one another in order to magnify all that we have in common, or almost all that we have in common, and recognize its meaning. So many problems are created for the Orthodox and Catholic churches in the world today, and they require so much adaptability on the parts of the two churches. Why should we not study them together and seek common solutions? If we did this, a sort of osmosis of mentalities would take effect, and, as time went on, if we allowed ourselves under the guidance of the Holy Spirit to approach possible solutions from deep within, then perhaps we would find solutions to the problems which separate us, for which we have apparently not yet been able to find answers. In any event, making progress is never an easy thing; it requires great demands of increasing magnitude as well as trust in the Lord and in His mysterious designs.

Question: Is concerted effort in preparing public opinion advantageous, and how should it be carried out?

Answer: It is more than advantageous, it is absolutely necessary. But here, too, we must avoid taking the line of least resistance. This is basically a question of Christian education, of deepening the Christian soul, of renewing Christian life. To prepare public opinion means first of all to draw attention to the major doctrines of the mystery of the Church which Christ created as a whole and unified entity. Moreover, this means instructing people to learn to know one another and treat each other as brothers. If only Catholics would acquire a knowledge of the true Christian life of their Orthodox brothers, and if only the Orthodox would acquaint themselves with that of their Catholic brothers! There are so many ways to do this: magazine

148

articles, study circles for members of the clergy and universities. We could think about pilgrimages to Jerusalem, Tinos, Patras, Lourdes, Rome, and we could meet one another in prayer. Each of us could, in turn, arrange lecture evenings at the point when we are spiritually equipped to take on such an endeavor; we could come to know one another, bear witness loyally and sincerely to what we are, and what we believe and think, and in doing so, protect ourselves from any atmosphere of propaganda or polemic apologetics. We must be willing to use all modern means of communication to further our growing acquaintanceship. The Italian television network recently offered a one-hour reportage on the Greek Orthodox church which was presented in a very congenial manner. This is just one example among many. It is of utmost importance for the public to understand and desire this rapprochement. This is the prerequisite for any true progress.

Question: Are systematic contacts between representatives of each of the churches and simple followers of other churches viewed as constructive, or should efforts toward rapprochement be carried out exclusively by the heads of churches?

Answer: I feel that the foregoing replies allow me to be brief here. If this is a question of resuming the habit of living together, then it requires contacts on the various levels of Church life. Obviously, the contacts established between the heads of churches do have the special significance I described in my reply to a previous question. But additional contacts are necessary, contacts which, to the extent that they correspond to the spirit of respect, love, loyalty, sincerity, and trust I have already alluded to in various instances, do not run the risk of leading either to indifference or to proselytism.

Question: What precise meaning does the Roman Catholic Church attribute to its request for an equitable dialogue with the Orthodox church? Could we look upon this request as one which could affect the primacy of the pope?

Answer: In its *Decree on Ecumenism* the Second Vatican Council clearly stated that this dialogue would have to be held on terms of equality. In No. 9 of this Decree, a dialogue is described as a conversation in which all participating parties consider themselves equals. Nothing should be excluded from this dialogue. But it should deal with all subjects in the proper spirit and with the proper preparation. It is a credit to the great wisdom of the Third Panorthodox Conference in Rhodes to have understood and comprehended this fact. There can be no other prerequisites for a dialogue than those of love, respect, sincerity, strength of mind, understanding, and the ability to listen to another. And we cannot omit any subject whatever from such a dialogue, for its very purpose is to overcome difficulties. Dialogue must allow us to open the door to acquisition of profound knowledge of one another. The dialogue on doctrine, which will be the second stage in our march forward, must be prepared with the greatest of care as far as the themes are concerned and as far as the participating parties are concerned. But here, too, it is primarily a question of spirit, and spirit here means the Spirit of Christ and His Gospel. If we are moved by this Spirit, He in turn will lead us, if such is His desire, towards the sort of unity He may desire by any means He may desire to use.

4. The Results and Effects of Discussions
Among Church Leaders

Question: In the opinion of Your Eminence, what is the import of this visit, and what are the concrete results and realistic prospects deriving from the conversations between Pope Paul VI and the Archbishop of Canterbury, and between yourself and Dr. Ramsey?

Answer: It is said, and I feel correctly so, that this visit has surpassed all expectations. Its significance lies mainly in the fact that it introduced a new and very fruitful stage in the development of brotherly relations between the English church, the Anglican community, and the Roman Catholic Church, and did so by means of an extensive, long-range program. Concrete results? First of all we should perhaps decide what we mean by concrete results and realistic prospects. For example, would you designate as a "concrete result" the joint declaration issued by the Holy Father and Patriarch Athenagoras by which the sad events surrounding the year 1054 were obliterated from the Church's memory? Naturally both the Council and public opinion throughout the entire world, one could say, attributed the greatest possible importance to these declarations. It is worth the effort to remind practical and technically-minded men of the 20th century of the worth of those intrinsic values; authentic and deep values, of course, as opposed to the superficial and ephemeral ones created by profit-conscious propaganda.

Question: Is Your Eminence perhaps alluding here to the joint declaration?

Answer: Yes, and primarily to the part where the Holy

151

Father and the president of the English congregation express the desire to wipe the past from their memories and try in the future to answer their Christian calling, in particular as far as love of one human being for another is concerned. This desire would gradually have to affect all members and all levels of the Catholic and Anglican churches down to the very last follower, and it would have to be translated into mutual respect and into effort towards learning to know one another and help one another to the best of one's ability. This is the basis for everything else.

Perhaps a comparison is necessary to shed light on the significance of this meeting. We will remember that Pope John XXIII, in his encyclical on peace, said that peace cannot be lasting when it is based solely on balance of power, fear, or mere agreements, and not on mutual trust. The same sort of idea applies to the area of ecumenicity. If the intention existed to maintain love at any price, there would not have been any separation. Therefore the first and foremost step towards unity is mutual, active love.

Question: Has this intention already enjoyed any special practical application of one sort or another?

Answer: Certainly. May I remind you once again of the step taken in the joint declaration issued by the Holy Father and the Archbishop which speaks of a dialogue based on the Gospel and other common ancient traditions in both churches which could lead to the unity in truth which Christ prayed for. Don't you also feel that this was the most extensive, profound, and truly Christian plan of action that could have been laid out in so few words?

Question: Your Eminence, could you describe for us in more precise terms the subjects to be dealt with in this dialogue?

Answer: We shall primarily have to treat subjects dealing with doctrine. The Declaration expressly mentions holy Scripture, tradition, and liturgy. But these are just a few examples. We can safely say that many different questions brought up at the Council could also be the object of our religious discussions. This applies, in particular, to Church teachings, divine revelation, bases for ecumenism, and religious freedom.

Then there would be questions of a practical nature, and first of all those which create the greatest difficulties. This category includes the complex of questions concerning mixed marriage, and the entire scale of questions involving modern religious welfare from all points of view, particularly those problems treated in the *Constitution on the Church in the Modern World, such as,* for example, the problems of conjugal love, culture, economic and social life, political coexistence on national and international levels, and especially the problem of peace. All of this puts us at a loss as to choosing and deciding which problems should be given priority.

Question: Your Eminence has just mentioned the problem of mixed marriage. How were the regulations recently issued by the Congregation of Faith on this subject accepted in Anglican circles?

Answer: I do not feel we can answer this question at the present time. You are aware, no doubt, that the document was made public just a few days ago. For this reason there has not yet been enough time to make the required fundamental study of the delicate material contained in it. Based on pertinent earlier declarations, one could, without difficulty, acquire some idea as to what fruits instruction has borne. Above all else I feel that those who look at things from an unbiased point of view will recognize that instruction provides a serious step forward, that is, a serious step towards adapting ourselves to the present-day situation. On the other hand, we certainly cannot expect instruction to bring complete satisfaction, for the solution it provides is one which it, itself, foresees as an experiment, that is, providing that the facts bear it out. It is also not surprising that many people are disappointed with one aspect or another. It goes without saying that further discussion will be helpful in producing a sense of rapprochement. However, we must admit in all frankness that no solution will be totally satisfactory in a certain sense. Mixed marriage, in particular, reveals the whole paradox of separation among Christians, which is the basis of its setbacks. The only valid solution would be reunification. Until such time the difficulties and the cross remain, and a great deal of patience and love are necessary.

Question: What is Your Eminence's opinion of the effect of this visit and these discussions on other separated Christians?

Answer: Experience shows that such meetings and examples of rapprochement between the various churches generally have a favorable influence on the issue of reunification. This is proved, for instance, by the results obtained by the aforementioned joint declaration issued by the Holy Father and the ecumenical patriarch of Constantinople last December. Even though in politics we fear that approaches made towards one party might result in alienation by others, in the Church of God all members are part of the same Mystical Body of which Christ is the Head, and any increase in love among individual members is of benefit to the other members and to the entire Body. In this sense the Archbishop of Canterbury's visit not only constitutes a significant contribution to ecumenism, but an outstanding service to the Church of Christ itself. The Church of England, the Anglican community, and, above all, the Giver of all that is good merit sincere gratitude for this.

VI.

Welcome Address

BY WILLEM A. VISSER 'T HOOFT

YOUR EMINENCE, President Boegner, Representatives of the Churches, of the Diplomatic Corps, and of the Government of Geneva, Ladies and Gentlemen*:

It is indeed a joy and an honor for the World Council of Churches to receive at its headquarters two men whose names are indissolubly linked both with the past history and with the present development of the Ecumenical Movement. The fact that we welcome at the same time His Eminence Cardinal Bea, director of the Secretariat for the Promotion of Christian Unity, and President Boegner, one of the founders of the World Council of Churches, speaks volumes in itself. And the moment at which we do so, namely a few months after the promulgation of the Vatican Council's *Decree on Ecumenism* and a few weeks after the declaration made by the Central Committee of our Council concerning the further pursuit of conversation with the Roman Catholic Church—this moment is singularly appropriate.

Our meeting could never have taken place without long and patient preparation. Our thoughts turn to those pioneers who had the courage to proclaim the unavoidable necessity of

* Address given at the reception for Augustin Cardinal Bea and Dr. Marc Boegner on February 18, 1966, at the Ecumenical Center in Geneva.

ecumenical endeavor at a time when the churches still lived in a state of almost complete isolation from one another. Dr. Boegner, you belong to the generation of those who strove for the ecumenical cause during the years when that cause seemed no more than a dream or an illusion. I have never forgotten how you guided the World Council during the years of the Second World War. It was thus entirely proper that it should have been you who presented, at Amsterdam in 1948, the resolution proposing the setting up of the World Council of Churches, and that the Assembly should have chosen you as the first European president of the Council.

During the years of preparation for the establishment of the Council, our activities were closely followed, or rather accompanied by a certain number of Roman Catholic ecumenists. They put to us questions which made us think. They compelled us, by their warnings and their constructive criticisms, to make clear our intentions. Their work contributed to the enrichment of the ecumenical conversation. It was during those days that we learned to know and to appreciate the man who is today Bishop Willebrands.

These contacts were valuable, but they lacked the mark of ecclesiastical sanction. We rejoiced all the more when Pope John XXIII decided to set up the Secretariat for the Promotion of Christian Unity. At last there was an address at Rome to which we could turn for the discussion of questions of common interest. And I must add, Your Eminence, that the spirit which you have caused to prevail in that Secretariat has greatly smoothed our path. The deep personal interest which you have shown in the development of good and close relations between your Secretariat and our Council, the manner in which you have greeted our invitations to you to send observers to our meetings, and above all the welcome which you have kindly extended to our observers at the Second Vatican Council: all these things have touched us profoundly. But more than this, it was your Secretariat upon whom fell the great and precious task of preparing the schema on ecumenism. We realize that this was no easy task. You were obliged to shoulder the burdens of the pioneer. But now that that schema has become a decree of the Vatican Council, you must allow us to say how much we honor the man who is its spiritual father. You are of course aware that we cannot subscribe to all the statements contained in the Decree, but we can fully appreciate what it means in the history of ecumenism. This is not the moment to say all that could be said concerning the conception of Ecumenism found in the *Decree on Ecumenism*. But I should like to emphasize two things which seem to me of special importance.

The first is the clear statement in the Decree that the future progress of ecumenism depends upon the renewal of the life of the Church, a renewal understood as an ever-growing faithfulness to her vocation. Here is a conviction which we can wholly share, for we have already discovered within the life of the WCC that churches are unable to advance towards unity unless they can free themselves from all that is foreign to their true nature and unless they allow themselves to be purified and renewed by the Holy Spirit and by the Word of God.

The Basis of the World Council speaks of "the common calling of the churches" which they "seek to fulfill together to the glory of the one God, Father, Son, and Holy Spirit." It is in obedience to this calling and in sharing the spiritual gifts accorded to each church that a common growth towards unity is achieved.

We are particularly happy that the Decree speaks of holy Scripture as an outstanding means, in the powerful hands of God, for obtaining that unity which our Saviour offers to mankind. For we believe that all those who devote themselves to the Scriptures, in a spirit of humility and obedience, hear the voice of God speaking to them there. We are also happy to think, Your Eminence, that the one who has been called to preside over the Secretariat for the Promoting of Christian Unity, has always been a student of the Bible and is indeed known as a most notable biblical scholar and teacher.

In the second place, we are glad to find that the Decree rejects any notion of "ecumenical confusion," and describes the ecumenical quest as a "loyal dialogue" in which genuine differences are taken with full seriousness.

Allow me at this point a remark concerning terminology. I have been struck by the fact that the Decree so often uses the words "nevertheless" (*nihilominus*) or "however" (*attamen*). And I think that this is good. For true ecumenism is indeed an attitude characterized by these two words. We do not minimize our differences, nor do we yet see how they could be reconciled. Ecumenism is not based upon the impression that our differences are in process of disappearing, but rather upon the conviction that, in spite of the differences, we must try constantly to speak, and if possible, to work, together. We then find that the differences are still there and as great as ever, yet we also say: "*nevertheless,*" since we believe in the same God, the same Saviour, the same Holy Spirit, we must seek to understand one another, we must try to live together as Christians ought to do.

The fact that we are now preparing to set up a working party, composed of representatives of the Roman Catholic Church and of the WCC, means that we wish to engage in a common exploration of the ways in which we can contribute to the establishment of closer relations with one another. It is not the role of the WCC to engage with the Roman Catholic Church upon negotiations concerning church union, but there are plenty of important questions which we could and should study together in order that we may give a positive direction to the development of ecumenism. We are thinking here both of those questions which have caused, and still do cause, severe tensions between the churches, and also of matters in which there is a real possibility of working together in the practical field. This we shall do with a sharp awareness of the spiritual and material situation of mankind as a whole. The common task of giving this world of ours the bread of life and bread to eat is one which surpasses the strength of us all, and it follows that we cannot afford the luxury of being in competition with each other when it comes to spreading the Gospel. In the world which is coming into being before our very eyes, the churches will not be able to help the nations in their spiritual and moral distress unless they are willing to work closely together. As stated in that very important schema on religious liberty produced by your Secretariat, the only means which the churches can and should use are means of a purely spiritual character, in other words the intrinsic power of the word of God. May it not be possible that in accepting the vocation of the Church to be a servant and no more than a servant, we may together be led into a deeper sense of brotherhood with one another?

President Boegner has written that there is not one cross for Protestants, another for Orthodox, another for Roman Catholics,

160

or, indeed, one for ecumenists. There is only the cross of Jesus Christ. He adds, "Whether the members of the divided churches wish it or not, this cross unites them."

It is because of this cross, set up by God at the center of history, that we can utter the "nevertheless" of faith, and in spite of all the tragic happenings which belong to the history of divided Christendom, can advance with confidence along the road of ecumenism.

Your Eminence, Dr. Boegner, we thank you with all our hearts for the honor that you have done us by paying us this visit, and we wish to express to you our respect and our fraternal greetings. Our good wishes go with you personally and with your service of the ecumenical cause.

VII.

The Church and Religious Freedom

BY AUGUSTIN CARDINAL BEA

THE VOTE TAKEN on September 21, 1965, which was correctly designated as a historical vote, concerned the question of whether or not the schema for the *Declaration on Religious Liberty* which had been discussed for several days could be accepted as the basis of the final Council Declaration. The decisive item on the agenda was the request to improve the schema "in accordance with Catholic doctrine on true religion." Then, when the revised text was distributed, and the introduction added to the schema precisely on the basis of this request was left as is (the most important ideas in it are presently to be found in No. 1 of the document), more than just a few persons were extremely concerned. They felt that any hasty assertions would ruin the entire Declaration. Others, non-Catholic Christians among them, gave this problem more careful thought. They were in agreement with the importance of such an addition. Furthermore, they pointed out the fact that in the non-Catholic ecumenical movement the necessity was repeatedly felt to stress the irrevocable obligation of man towards the truth of Christ in face of any type of passive consent or religious indifference. On the other hand, the group of those who were perturbed interpreted this as a mere "customary" compromise by which a "progressive" document was designed to gratify the "conservative" wing, or, in other words, by which conservative elements were, by necessity, being affirmed in addition to modern ones. Where does the truth lie? Does this concern a superficial compromise only, or does it mean something else?

In order to answer this question, let us first look squarely at the facts on which the Council document is based and which are clearly indicated therein in various passages. In this Declaration, too, the Council bears witness to the fixing of its spiritual goal: One must look at the truths of today's world and base oneself on them in order to be able to serve contemporary men.

1. The Point of Departure

One of the first factors to be taken into consideration is modern man's struggle for freedom. The document emphasizes this from the very begining: "A sense of dignity of the human person has been impressing itself more and more deeply on the consciousness of contemporary man. And the demand is increasingly made that men should act on their own judgment, enjoying and making use of a responsible freedom, not driven by coercion but motivated by a sense of duty" (No. 1). This demand for freedom is especially directly towards "the quest for the values proper to the human spirit . . . in the first place, the free exercise of religion in society." For this reason the demand is made for "constitutional limits" to be "set to the powers of government, in order that there may be no encroachment on the rightful freedom of the person and of associations" (*ibid.*). This is especially necessary since the Council must confirm "with great sorrow" that "forms of government still exist under

which, even though freedom of religious worship receives constitutional recognition, the powers of government are engaged
in the effort to deter citizens from the profession of religion
and to make life difficult and dangerous for religious communities" (No. 15).

A second series of facts concerns the general condition of
contemporary man. For it is obvious that "all nations are coming
into even closer unity. Men of different cultures and religions
are being brought together in closer relationships. There is a
growing consciousness of the personal responsibility that weighs
upon every man" (No. 15). Such unity must, of course, be
brought about in an atmosphere of harmony and peace and
this can only be attained if we guarantee all people their well-
deserved religious freedom together with all rights and privileges
resulting therefrom.

A third series of facts concerns the Church and her mission.
God did not abandon man in his quest for Him. Instead, He
revealed himself to mankind, showed it the way towards salvation through Christ, and appointed the Church as custodian of
the revelation for man (No. 1). In view of these realities, the
document sets forth the basic concept of religious liberty, explains
what it implies and what it must accomplish, shows the necessity for education in freedom and its ultimate goal, and finally
speaks of the obligations which devolve upon Church members
in this regard.

2. The Basic Concept

We now want to see how the Council reacts and replies to
these facts and the problems connected with them. In view of
contemporary man's striving towards freedom, the Council pro-

poses to declare it "to be greatly in accord with truth and justice" (No. 1). To that end the Council looks at human nature in the light of reason (in order to be understood also by those who do not share in Christ's mission), and searches into "the sacred tradition and doctrine of the Church—the treasury out of which the Church continually brings forth new things that are in harmony with the things that are old" (*ibid.*).

How is this demand for freedom found deep within the human spirit interpreted? The Council replies: "It is in accordance with their dignity as persons—that is, as beings endowed with reason and free will and therefore privileged to bear personal responsibility—that all men should be at once impelled by nature and also bound by a moral obligation to seek the truth, especially religious truth. They are also bound to adhere to the truth, once it is known, and to order their whole lives in accord with the demands of truth" (No. 2). After the document thus confirms the essential relationship between freedom and truth, it continues as follows: "However, men cannot discharge these obligations in a manner in keeping with their own nature unless they enjoy immunity from external coercion as well as psychological freedom" (*ibid.*).

These fundamental ideas show clearly what the true aims of freedom are. Freedom is not and cannot be arbitrary or changeable, and even less can it result from mere external pressure (as we often see it today). Freedom strives essentially to acquire and enjoy truth, and life led according to the truth.[1]

The Council then deals with individual questions. It examines and clarifies another basic element of freedom, freedom from external pressure, which, indeed "means that all men are to be

1. In this connection see the *Pastoral Constitution on the Church in the Modern World*, No. 17.

immune from coercion on the part of individuals or of social groups and of any human power, in such wise that in matters religious no one is to be forced to act in a manner contrary to his own beliefs. Nor is anyone to be restrained from acting in accordance with his own beliefs, whether privately or publicly, whether alone or in association with others, within due limits" (No. 2).

In this connection the Church powerfully and clearly resolved the long-disputed issue of the right to freedom for those who have gone astray. Until a very few years ago it was extremely difficult even to prove the existence of such a right for those who erred, but who did so in good faith.[2]

But the Council goes above and beyond this point and declares that ". . . the right to this immunity continues to exist even in those who do not live up to their obligation of seeking the truth and adhering to it. Nor is it the exercise of this right to be impeded, provided that the just requirements of public order are observed" (No. 2). In other words, this right is reserved in its entirety even for the person who does not commit his error in good faith, and it is reserved under the exact same conditions of respect for public order which apply to the exercise of any right, as we shall see right away. The Council document offers an unequivocally clear argument to the effect that a right such as this "has its foundation not in the subjective disposition of the person, but in his very nature" (*ibid.*); it can therefore not be alienated on the basis of any specific subjective conditions which do not and cannot modify the nature of man.

As we have already said, the Council demonstrates that the doctrine of man's right to religious freedom "has its foundation

2. See Augustin Cardinal Bea, "Religiöse Freiheit und Wandlungen der Gesellschaft," in *Stimmen der Zeit* 173 (1963/64), 321.

in the very dignity of the human person, as this dignity is known through the revealed word of God and by reason itself" (No. 2). It views the nature of the relationship between man and God in a special way, and derives the following rule from it for the attitude of governments towards religious freedom: "The religious acts whereby men, in private and in public and out of a sense of personal conviction, direct their lives to God transcend by their very nature the order of terrestrial and temporal affairs" (No. 3). Based on this viewpoint the document arrives at the following conclusive principle: "Government, therefore, ought indeed to take account of the religious life of the people and show it favor, since the function of government is to make provision for the common welfare. However, it would clearly transgress the limit set to its power were it to presume to direct or inhibit acts that are religious" (*ibid.*).

As far as the proofs of revelation are concerned, the Declaration concedes that "revelation does not indeed affirm in so many words the right of man to immunity from external coercion in matters religious" (No. 9). But the document does stress the fact that it discloses "the dignity of the human person in its full dimensions. It gives evidence of the respect which Christ showed towards the freedom with which man is to fulfill his duty of believing in the word of God. It gives us lessons, too, in the spirit which disciples of such a Master ought to make their own and to follow in every situation" (*ibid.*). The Declaration therefore seeks to intensify these general observations and analyze the freedom which is proper to the practice of the Christian faith: "It is one of the major tenets of Catholic doctrine that man's response to God in faith must be free. Therefore, no one is to be forced to embrace the Christian faith against his own will. This doctrine is contained in the word

167

of God and it was constantly proclaimed by the Fathers of the Church" (No. 10).[3]

After analyzing in detail the above attitudes on the part of Christ and the apostles, the Council concludes that the doctrine by which the Church, in this document, "recognizes and gives support to the principle of religious freedom as befitting the dignity of man and as being in accord with divine revelation," represents an expression of the Church's trust in "the truth of the Gospel" and in the "way of Christ and the apostles" (No. 12). This is a doubly important conclusion. It pacifies, above all, those followers for whom the teachings in this document might occasionally appear modern and not too faithful to past tradition, and it also puts the entire weight of the Church's two thousand years of authoritative tradition to the service of defending the religious freedom which has been suppressed or diminished today in so many parts of the world.

3. Additional Conclusions

After substantiating the basic right to religious freedom in this way, the document goes on to explain the various aspects and consequences of it. A brief indication is sufficient here. In the first place, this concerns the freedom of religious communities. Just as these communities are "a requirement of the social nature both of man and of religion itself" (No. 4), the same

3. Reflecting on the history of the People of God, the Declaration frankly and honestly observes the following: "In the life of the People of God as it has made its pilgrim way through the vicissitudes of human history, there have at times appeared ways of acting which were less in accord with the spirit of the Gospel and even opposed to it. Nevertheless the doctrine of the Church that no one is to be coerced into faith has always stood firm." (No. 12)

holds true for their freedom. And such a right to freedom not only pertains to worship and all that is connected with worship (choice of office holders and their training, property, free association with followers from other countries, etc.), but also the right "not to be hindered in their public teaching and witness to their faith, whether by the spoken or by the written word" (*ibid.*). Here, of course, we immediately strike on the standard of respect paid towards the rights of others, a standard which must be observed in the exercise of religious freedom exactly as it must be in the exercise of any other right. By virtue of this standard "everyone ought at all times to refrain from any manner of action which might seem to carry a hint of coercion or of a kind of persuasion that would be dishonorable or unworthy, especially when dealing with poor or uneducated people" (*ibid.*). It is not difficult to recognize the significance of this standard, not only in order to avoid dangers, but also to dispel any fears which the use of this right to religious freedom might allow to arise occasionally for those concerned with the spiritual welfare of others.

That which has been said about the right of religious communities to religious freedom applies starting from the very first moment of man's life in a social setting, in the family: it applies to domestic religious life, upbringing of children, freedom in selection of school, etc. (No. 5).

4. Incorporation of Religious Freedom into Society

Just as the social nature of religion automatically implies rights for religious communities as such, it also requires that the use of freedom (from the point of view of the individual or of social groups) be applied to the whole of society, in particular to the type of society called a "welfare" society. This requires, on the one hand, protection of the rights of persons and communities, and, on the other hand, respect for the limitations imposed on the use of freedom so that it remains in harmony with the whole of life in society.

This concerns, above all, putting freedom to use for the purpose of public welfare. This concept is paraphrased as follows in our document: "The common welfare of society consists in the entirety of those conditions of social life under which men enjoy the possibility of achieving their own perfection in a certain fullness of measure and also with some relative ease. Hence, this welfare consists chiefly in the protection of the rights, and in the performance of the duties of the human person" (No. 6). On the basis of such a statement, one can immediately arrive at the conclusion that responsibility for religious freedom and its appropriate use for the common good are not only incumbent upon public authority, as was frequently thought. Instead, they are a result of concerted effort by all parties concerned: "Therefore, the care of the right to religious freedom devolves upon the people as a whole, upon social groups, upon government, and upon the Church and other religious Communities, in virtue of the duty of all towards the common welfare, and in the manner proper to each" (*ibid.*).

In contributing to the preservation of religious freedom, both individual persons and social groups must, above all, adhere to regulatory norms applicable to the exercise of each and every personal social responsibility, namely, they are all obligated to "have respect both for the rights of others and for their own duties towards others and for the common welfare of all. Men are to deal with their fellows in justice and civility" (No. 7).

In addition to this, there is the protective norm of so-called "public order." Since, however, according to our Declaration, responsibility for such protection lies mainly with governments, special consideration is then given to the duties of public authorities.

Delineation of the duties of public authorities is based on the general principle already stated to the effect that government must respect and promote the religious life of its citizens and that it ought not to presume to direct or inhibit acts that are religious (No. 3). "Promote" here means that "government is to assume the safeguard of the religious freedom of all its citizens, in an effective manner, by just laws and by other appropriate means. Government is also to help create conditions favorable to the fostering of religious life, in order that the people may be truly enabled to exercise their religious rights and to fulfill their religious duties . . ." (No. 6). The deeper motive for this obligation is not only the responsibility of civil authorities towards individual citizens. It is also a responsibility towards the welfare of society itself so that "society itself may profit by the moral qualities of justice and peace which have their origin in men's faithfulness to God and to His holy will" (No. 16).

In this connection, the Declaration then deals with the specific case where "in view of peculiar circumstances obtaining among certain peoples, special legal recognition is given in the constitutional order of society to one religious body . . ." (No. 6). What is government's obligation in such a case as far as other citizens and other religious groups are concerned? ". . . [I]t is at the same time imperative that the right of all citizens and religious bodies to religious freedom should be recognized and made effective in practice." Therefore, no special favors should

171

be granted to one social group at the expense of the rights of any other persons or social groups. The Declaration emphasizes this point more expressly in another sentence. "Finally, the government is to see to it that the equality of citizens before the law, which is itself an element of the common welfare, is never violated for religious reasons whether openly or covertly. Nor is there to be discrimination among citizens" (*ibid.*). If, then, discrimination of any type is so vigorously repudiated, it is even more serious when governments combat religions as such, as has unfortunately happened in the past, and as happens still today. The Declaration denounces such conduct as being "a violation of the will of God and of the sacred rights of the person and the family of nations . . ." (*ibid.*).

One last important point is that of society's protection against possible disturbances to its public order. This protection "is the special duty of government." But public order is "genuine public peace, which comes about when men live together in good order and in true justice" and it is "proper guardianship of public morality" (No. 7). It is easy to see that this norm for public order is only too susceptible to abuse. For this reason the Declaration immediately elucidates its nature and limitations. As far as the nature of public order is concerned, protection from disturbances to this order should not take place "in arbitrary fashion or in an unfair spirit of partisanship. Its action is to be controlled by juridical norms which are in conformity with the objective moral order. These norms arise out of the need for effective safeguard of the rights of all citizens and for peaceful settlement of conflicts of rights." On the other hand, the following principle applies to the limitations of the norm regulating public order: "For the rest, the usages of society are to be the usages of freedom in their full range. These require that the freedom of man be respected as far as possible, and curtailed only when and insofar as necessary" (*ibid.*).

5. Educating for Freedom

Everything that has been stated thus far about the rights of religious communities, the exercise of freedom in society, and the common welfare and public order essentially concerns that aspect of religious freedom defined at the outset as "freedom from coercion." Though this concept may seem empty and purely negative, the Declaration, by means of its rich content and multiple conclusions, nevertheless demonstrates its powerful significance, and, above all, its appropriateness in today's world. However, we must admit that this concept indicates a more external aspect of religious freedom, namely, protection of such freedom from outside. The Council was well aware of this. We need only bear in mind the fact that several Council Fathers insisted on the necessity of education in exercising freedom, and on proper and sincere use of this great gift of God.

What special conditions of our time require such education? There are special dangers which threaten today's freedom. The Declaration explains that "Many pressures are brought to bear upon men of our day, to the point where the danger arises that they lose the possibility of acting on their own judgment" (No. 8). Upon closer examination of these ideas and other references in the Declaration we can discern a few fundamental principles. The manifold and increasingly closer relationships between men of different cultures and religions (No. 15) lead all too easily to the idea that peaceful, harmonious coexistence is better assured when the question of truth is not posed at all, but when one admits that all religions are equally good if only men would live them sincerely and seriously. And it would be even worse if, when subjected to the most varied types of influences, freedom would be understood as completely independent of any moral order or authority.[4] The powerful instruments of communication also create the danger of leveling off the true independence of man and his judgment in his quest for truth and in his quest to reach personal decisions, in that men are thereby reduced to an amorphous mass, deprived of the "possibility of action on their own judgment."[5] These are just a few allusions to the grave dangers which threaten to impair, if not altogether to destroy man's true freedom generally, and more specifically, the freedom most sacred to him, freedom in his religious life.

For this reason the *Declaration on Religious Liberty* makes its strongest appeal to educators, above all others. This appeal is so essential that we must reiterate it in its entirety. Educators should do their utmost, explains the Declaration, to "form men who will respect the moral order and be obedient to lawful authority. Let them form men, too, who will be lovers of true freedom—men, in other words, who will come to decisions on their own judgment and in the light of truth, govern their activities with a sense of responsibility, and strive after what is true and right, willing always to join with others in cooperative effort" (No. 8).

4. See No. 8 plus the *Pastoral Constitution on the Church in the Modern World,* Nos. 17 and 20.

5. No. 8. Also see the *Decree on the Instruments of Social Communication,* Nos. 4, 8, 10, 12. In connection with this problem also see A. Cardinal Bea, *Einheit in Freiheit* (Stuttgart 1965) p. 39.

6. The Final Goal

But this is not all. We must bear in mind the last of the three categories mentioned at the outset, namely that the way to achieve true union with God Himself was revealed to man in Christ, and that the Church is the teacher of this way through the will of God and Christ. This is why the Church feels obligated to lead its followers along the precarious road to freedom, that is, to free acceptance of the truth and its realization. Indeed, if the Church had not spoken to its followers in such a special way, then they would not have had a reply as to what was to be derived from the Declaration for their own lives. Many people would have been surprised if the Church had spoken about obligations towards truth merely in a general manner, without bearing witness to the truth entrusted to it by Christ; that is, if it had spoken as if it were not sure of its own mission, or as if it wanted to deny this mission. For this reason the Declaration specifies the fact that those who recognize and acknowledge the truth revealed by God and the Church's holy mission are under obligation to remain faithful to the Church, study it, grow progressively more acquainted with it, spread it, and profess it "even to the shedding of their blood" (No. 14), if such proves necessary.

But the Church also knows that it is obligated towards those who are not yet aware of Christianity as the one true religion and who do not yet understand the holy mission of the Church. By virtue of its mission and its love towards these individuals, it knows it is duty bound to lead them towards the goal of freely seeking and accepting the truth, and also to show them the entire truth which God bestowed upon humanity through

175

Christ. This is the sole purpose of the Introduction, which, as we have already noted, proved to be such a disappointment to several people. It commences with the solemn words: "First, this sacred Synod professes its belief that God Himself has made known to mankind the way in which men are to serve Him, and thus be saved in Christ and come to blessedness. We believe that this one true religion subsists in the Catholic and apostolic Church, to which the Lord Jesus committed the duty of spreading it abroad among all men" (No. 1).

7. Freedom of the Church

The same consciousness of its own mission and the same view towards its own followers and towards those who are not, leads the Church, in this document, to claim the freedom owed to it, that is, as a community and by virtue of the special task entrusted to it by Christ. Accordingly, it relies in a most unique way on the title of freedom bestowed upon it by Christ, and considers this freedom "sacred because the only-begotten Son endowed with it the Church which He purchased with His blood" (No. 13). Furthermore, it affirms that freedom is owed to it on the basis of its "character as a spiritual authority, established by Christ the Lord. Upon this authority there rests, by divine mandate, the duty of going out into the whole world and preaching the gospel to every creature" (*ibid.*). And this freedom of the Church "is the fundamental principle in what concerns the relations between the Church and governments and the whole civil order" (*ibid.*).

However, the Church's claim to a special right of freedom does not mean that it demands an exceptional position for itself; it demands for itself no greater freedom, in the sense of freedom

176

from coercion and pressure, than that which is dealt with in the first part of the Council document. Emphasis is therefore not placed on its rights at the expense of equality of rights of other communities. This is most clearly elucidated in what the Council Declaration sets forth concerning practical realization of the Church's right to freedom, namely that in those places where general freedom of religion reigns, the Church, too, enjoys the freedom it needs: "In turn, where the principle of religious freedom is not only proclaimed in words or simply incorporated in law but also given sincere and practical application, there the Church succeeds in achieving a stable situation of right as well as of fact and the independence which is necessary for the fulfillment of her divine mission. This independence is precisely what the authorities of the Church claim in society" (No. 13). This part of the Declaration therefore correctly concludes:[6] "Therefore, a harmony exists between the freedom of the Church and the religious freedom which is to be recognized as the right of all men and communities and sanctioned by constitutional law" (ibid.).[7]

8. The Duty of Church Members

Finally, the Church is urged, through the consciousness of its duty to safeguard spiritual welfare, to indicate to Catholic followers the way they must behave towards non-Catholic Chris-

6. The following sentence is missing in the text distributed by the Catholic News Agency and it is therefore missing in almost all of the translations published to date in Germany. The only version here which is reliable is the one issued on December 7, 1965 by the Council Press Office in conjunction with the Secretariat for Promoting Christian Unity.

7. See, in connection with this difficult question, J. Courtney Murray, "Osservazioni sulla Dichiarazione sulla Libertà Religiosa," in La Civiltà Cattolica, 1965 I 536–554, especially p. 544.

tians, non-Christians, and non-believers in carrying out the principles set forth in this Declaration. In point of fact, the Council knows that the Church's deportment is clearly formed both in its members' attitude and by means of their attitude; in other words, primarily by its bishops and their associates in the priesthood, and also by laymen. But this realization places the followers of Christ before the same problem with which the Council was also faced in dealing with it. The problem is to coordinate the principle of respect for the dignity and freedom of man with the principle of fidelity to the preaching of Christ's mission, as it was received from Him. Such fidelity is demanded by our true love towards mankind as well. It induces Church members to impart to other men, to the fullest extent possible, the treasures they have received from God for the welfare of all men, for the welfare of all humanity.

Therefore, the basic principle from which the attitude of the Church's followers must emanate is: "All is to be taken into account—the Christian duty to Christ, the life-giving word which must be proclaimed, the rights of the human person . . ." (No. 14). In the meantime, Church members must "walk in wisdom in the face of those outside, 'in the Holy Spirit, in un-affected love, in the word of truth' (2 Cor. 6, 6–7). Let them be about their task of spreading the light of life with all confidence and apostolic courage, even to the shedding of their blood" (*ibid*). However, this must be done with full respect for freedom, "never—be it understood—having recourse to means that are incompatible with the spirit of the Gospel." Indeed, the follower of Christ is urged to "act lovingly, prudently, and patiently in his dealings with those who are in error or ignorance with regard to the faith" (*ibid.*). The Declaration then adds the profound theological principle that men must heed "the measure of grace granted by God through Christ to men, who are invited freely to accept and profess the faith" (*ibid.*).

We have illustrated, by means of these practical guidelines, the special meaning the Declaration has for priests whose concern is the spiritual welfare of mankind. For the priest is the first teacher to instruct Christian followers on proper and full use of the sacred gift of freedom. Their personal and progressively more profound knowledge of the truth revealed by Christ is acquired when they learn how to form their own consciences in the light of this truth, and when they learn to accept this revealed truth freely and in the fullness of their hearts. They will thus be prepared to participate in the Church's holy mission themselves, this holy mission being to defend men's freedom[8] and preach the truth of Christ in order to lead other men as well towards cultivation of a proper attitude towards the most sacred thing which man possesses, his inner personal relationship with God—and all this with complete respect for man's freedom and with a view towards the measure of grace which each has received from Christ.

If, once again, we call to mind our point of departure in this study we shall then be able to state, in light of the commentaries we have just set forth, that the *Declaration on Religious Liberty,* far from being a flat compromise, represents an all-encompassing reply on the part of the Council to contemporary man's striving towards freedom, namely to his desire,

8. Also see the Council Decree's recommendation on the bishops' pastoral commitment: The Bishops "should give support to the principle of religious freedom as befitting the dignity of man . . . ".

motivated by consciousness of duty, to act on his own initiative. It desires to protect this freedom and to defend it against any coercion, unfair pressure, or interference which may arise. Further, it clarifies the true nature and aim of freedom, to the extent that such represents a freely undertaken search for, acceptance of and realization of truth. The Declaration, in conclusion, deals with the ultimate goal of freedom: the bringing about of man's union with God which, in itself, corresponds to the complete reality of man and his relationship to God, a relationship revealed in Christ through God Himself, and which constitutes the highest state of nobility and the greatest happiness of man throughout time and eternity.

VIII.

The Task of the Churches in the New Ecumenical Situation

BY WILLEM A. VISSER 'T HOOFT

THE CHURCHES' ECUMENICAL movement has entered a new phase of its history. Perhaps it could be called the phase of universality. The new thing about it is that all the large Christian churches are now participating in the ecumenical dialogue, and realize that they all have a special task to fulfill in this sphere.

The ecumenical movement had been started by the Protestant and Anglican churches in Europe and North America, and by the Greek-speaking Orthodox Churches. At that time the churches of Asia and Africa were not yet autonomous. The churches of Russia were completely cut off from the rest of the world. The Roman Catholic Church refused to participate, and criticized ecumenism as a sort of syncretism. At that time the ecumenical movement was far from being really ecumenical in the literal sense of the word. The Stockholm Conference in 1925 was therefore dominated by a purely western debate between the American "Social Gospel" theology and the eschatological theology of the German churches.

Shortly before the Second World War the Churches of Asia and Africa began to play an active part in the movement. The Conference of the International Missionary Council held at

Tambaram in 1939 was attended by as many delegates from the younger churches as from those in the west. Then when the countries of Africa and Asia became independent, and autonomous churches were formed everywhere which were fully aware of their special task within their own culture, ecumenism became *intercontinental*. The participation of the Orthodox churches—which at that time was important from the symbolic aspect but in actual fact was not at all active—became much more effective when in 1961 the churches of Russia, Romania, Bulgaria, and later the church of Yugoslavia joined the World Council of Churches. Ecumenism thereby finally lost its western character. For the first time since the schism a thousand years ago, it was possible to start a dialogue between eastern Christendom and western Christendom. But the largest Christian Church of all still held aloof. Admittedly a certain number of Catholic ecumenists followed the development of ecumenism with sympathy, and by their questions and advice helped in a very useful way to develop the ecumenical idea. But it was not until John XXIII became pope that the Roman Catholic Church as such developed any real ecumenical activity. This situation was changed by the Second Vatican Council. By setting up the Secretariat for Christian Unity, by inviting other churches to send observers, by the position of these observers in the life of the Council, by the *Decree on Ecumenism,* and by the ecumenical perspectives opened up in other decisions of the Council, the Catholic Church became actively involved in ecumenical activities. The Roman Church had traveled a long way since 1928, the year of the encyclical *Mortalium animos*. Archbishop Söderblom, to whom this encyclical was a great disappointment, certainly never ventured to hope that in 1964 a Council of the

Catholic Church would say that it welcomed the ecumenical movement and urged Catholics to respond to its call.

We have thus reached one of the aims set up by the pioneers of the ecumenical movement. All the Christian churches are to enter into conversation with each other, they are no longer to live in isolation, they are to realize that the cause of Christ transcends the boundaries of their own institutional life, they are to discover their solidarity, to cooperate in common tasks, and to seek together for ways which lead to full unity.

We are therefore living in a historic hour for the churches. Henceforth all the churches are obliged to get to know one another. They are making discoveries. They are astonished to see what they can learn from each other. They have to answer the questions put to them by their sister churches. They have to rethink many positions which are no longer in accordance with the new situation, to formulate them afresh or even to revise them.

Does this mean that we are living at a moment when ecumenism is triumphant? Certainly not. For the ultimate aim of the movement is not dialogue; it is genuine unity. Our Lord did not pray that they might all enter into conversation with each other; he prayed that they might all be one. We have no reason to be proud of ourselves just because we are beginning to explore ways which lead to unity. We ought to have done that long ago. We ought to have been ashamed that we so easily accepted the division which has characterized our behavior for so long.

Everything, or nearly everything, still remains to be done. No solution has yet been found to any of the great problems that exist between the churches. We have not yet made much progress in the question of intercommunion. Certain confessional positions are defended more obstinately today than when ecumenism was in its infancy. The Second Vatican Council has clearly stated that the decisions of 1870 concerning the infallibility of the pope and his universal jurisdiction—decisions which present an insuperable obstacle to the other churches—still retain their full weight.

We have therefore reached a dangerous point. We all want to be ecumenical, and we all want unity, but shall we succeed in carrying it out in practice? Or will it be said of our generation that all we did was to make pleasant speeches, but that we did not achieve anything new? Will the ecumenical dynamism of our time have to be compared with a horse that gallops up to an obstacle and then shirks the jump?

The question is all the more serious because the churches are placed in a world which tends more and more to think that it does not need the Church in order to arrange its own life. Churches which claim to possess the message of reconciliation, but which are not reconciled with one another, churches which profess to know the secret of a society based on justice and harmony, but which cannot agree to speak with a single voice, will not be able to arrest the process of de-Christianization which is gaining ground, despite all the churches' attempts to stop it. But this world of ours, which thinks it can get along perfectly well by itself, shows through its disorder, its incapacity to solve the most burning human problems, and its despair, that it needs the message of the renewal of all things in Christ more than ever before. The churches must all unite in bringing this message to the world.

What are the tasks of the churches in face of the new situation? In order to be able to answer this question we must first agree about the lessons to be learned from the past. During the short history of ecumenism, we have already learned some basic truths which should guide us during the years to come. I am thinking especially of the four following insights:

1. All ecumenism that is worthy of the name is a movement of concentration, a return to the sources, or still better a return to the center. This truth had been perceived already right at the beginning of the ecumenical movement. The message of the Stockholm Conference in 1925 said, "The nearer we come to the crucified Christ, the nearer we come to one another." But the consequences of this statement were not yet realized. It was not until 1952 at the World Conference of Faith and Order at Lund that the decision was taken to stop merely drawing comparisons between the differences in the different doctrinal questions, and in future to concentrate the theological work on the central theme "Christ and the Church." The whole life of the ecumenical movement shows that we can make progress only by carefully studying the Gospel of Jesus Christ together. It is no coincidence that the ecumenical movement was founded at the same time as a genuine renaissance in biblical theology. This theology, which quickened the life of many churches and showed that Christ himself is the center of Scripture, also lent its substance to the ecumenical dialogue.

It is therefore a very hopeful sign that, in its definition of ecumenism, the Vatican Council speaks the same language. I am thinking especially of the following passage: "When comparing doctrines [Catholic theologians] should remember that in Catholic teaching there exists an order or 'hierarchy' of truths, since they vary in their relationship to the foundation of the

Christian faith. Thus the way will be opened for this kind of 'fraternal rivalry' to incite all to a deeper realization and a clearer expression of the unfathomable riches of Christ."* Commenting on this passage in the *Decree on Ecumenism,* Cardinal Jaeger quotes the fine words of the Archbishop of Gorizia in the discussion on the schema: "It would be advisable to mention the center to which these elements [that is, the 'ecclesiastical realities' in the different churches and Christian communities] must be related and without which they cannot be understood. This link, this center, is Jesus Christ himself, whom all Christians recognize as Lord of the Church." I am convinced that the whole future of ecumenism depends on our loyalty to this fundamental principle. The ecumenical movement is christocentric, or else it is nothing at all. If we place ourselves under the authority of Jesus Christ we can rest assured that he will help us to accomplish his work of gathering together all who belong to him. It is he alone who brings vitality and momentum to us in our situation and gives us the renewal without which unity is not worth achieving.

2. The second lesson to be learned from the past is that fraternal relations based on confidence can be established only between churches which restrict themselves to spiritual methods in their action and in their relations with other churches. It is interesting to note that the problem of religious liberty has played a very important role in the discussions ever since the ecumenical movement began. Was this a concern for the interests of certain religious minorities in countries where a different confession or religion had a strong majority? Yes, but it was more than that. The profound mistrust between the churches

* *Decree on Ecumenism,* No. 11.

sprang from painful experiences in the past, in a great many cases memories of the political suppression of religious movements or of whole churches, sometimes even involving the use of force. The worst factors of division between the western and eastern Churches, between the Catholic Church and the Protestants, between the state churches and the so-called free churches were not of a dogmatic nature; they consisted in the use of non-spiritual methods to defend the power of the strongest church in this or that country. These fears had to be removed. Once and for all it had to be made clear that that time was over; from now on we completely reject all forms of coercion or power-policy. The only form of competition that we can accept is a purely spiritual one. We will no longer dream of restoring a Christianity which is under the jurisdiction of this or that individual church—a church which jealously defends its monopoly. We are ready to accept pluralism, not in the sense of a general indifferentism, but in the sense of a culture which permits the open expression of all serious convictions. Hence the consensus between the churches belonging to the World Council of Churches (who have discussed this question so frankly at their assemblies) and the Roman Catholic Church (which has just accepted the noteworthy *Decree on Religious Liberty*) is a good augury for the future of ecumenism. From now on it must be possible to eliminate the false elements, namely a policy of coercion and state intervention in purely religious questions. We consent to competition, to the struggle for truth, and to theological controversy. For the churches cannot lightly abandon a truth which they believe they have *received,* and not invented themselves. But all that must be done with complete freedom. Only in this way can all the Christian churches insist that in the countries dominated by Marxist ideology or by other religions Christians may be free to develop their own church life, with everything that is essential for the life of a Christian church.

3. We have also learned a third thing. In this world the churches have a task that is twofold. They are placed in this world to serve it and also to watch over it. One of the great motives for creating the ecumenical movement was the fact that the churches were no longer fulfilling their creative, dynamic task in our civilization. Söderblom was dismayed that the churches during the First World War were unable to speak and act as a firm supranational fellowship. He also realized the tremendous responsibility of the churches in face of the de-Christianization of the working classes and the success of anti-religious ideologies. The whole attitude of the churches to modern society must be thought out afresh, and they must learn to be present in that society in a new way, namely in the same way as the Lord of the Church—once again in the form of a servant. At the same time, however, one must learn afresh what was meant by the role of prophet as described by the prophet Ezekiel—namely the role of watchman who issues his warnings to the people as the mouthpiece of God. The churches had to learn to cooperate in service to their neighbor; they had to learn how to speak with a single voice to the world concerning the great problems of human life. It is true to say that this necessity of making a common witness to the world through word and deed was one of the strongest factors in the development of the ecumenical movement. We have no reason to feel satisfied with what the churches have been able to do to help mankind to solve its worst problems. But it is no small thing that churches

in the most widely differing national, racial, and ideological environments, churches so different from each other, have been able to show that the Church does not belong to the powers of this world but to the Lord, who is also the Servant of all men.

The Catholic Church has never ceased speaking to the world. In doing so, however, it often gave the impression that it wanted to lead people back to the time of the "corpus christianum," namely to a time when the Church was the supreme power and dominated society. It is therefore a very important thing that in its Pastoral Constitution *Gaudium et Spes* (the well-known Schema 13) the Vatican Council has spoken as a Church which on the one hand believes it has received the word of life for the whole world and for the whole of life, but on the other hand instead of condemning the modern world or wanting to dominate it desires to understand and serve it. This document had to be drawn up in record time and to deal with a large number of tremendous problems, and it does not contain very clear answers to the questions of our time. The important point, however, is that here the Catholic Church speaks a new language and adopts a new attitude towards the world. In this way all the churches find a common basis for their action in the world.

4. The past has taught us a fourth lesson. The only kind of ecumenism which has any future is an ecumenism which takes the churches seriously. You will say, that is self-evident. But today we see all kinds of tendencies at work, wanting to create an ecumenism which takes very little account of the existing churches. I would be the last person to criticize a spontaneous ecumenism of this kind. I realize only too well what the ecumenical movement of the churches owes to the pioneers, espe-

189

cially in the Christian youth movements, who prepared the way at a time when the churches were still deaf to the call to unity. Nor should it be forgotten that the Vatican Council's *Decree on Ecumenism* is the fruit of at least thirty years' work in small private groups in which Catholics and Protestants met for study. Fr. Congar has recently told the story of this spiritual adventure. But it was characteristic of these initiatives that they were taken in order to serve the churches and in the hope that they would follow them up. And so they did. It is not true that nothing can change in the great institutions of the churches. Admittedly, progress is slow and it is easy to lose one's patience. It is true also that at certain moments one must venture to raise opposition. But that opposition must be loyal and constructive. Our aim is not to create a new ecumenical sect, but to bring the churches in which and through which we have received our faith to unity.

What are the tasks of the churches in this new ecumenical situation? Let us begin with the tasks which the churches share in the world. As we have already seen, our generation has completely new opportunities in this respect. During the last few years we have had to learn some important lessons, and we are now beginning to see the possibility of joint action by the churches in the world. We are already in agreement that this action must not be ecclesiocentric, it must not be defensive, it must not try to turn the clock back. It must rather spring from a deep solidarity with all men, and especially with all who are underprivileged. It must seek justice for all and reconciliation between all, and the weapons which it uses must be exclusively spiritual in giving its prophetic message and passing on its convictions.

We have arrived at similar positions with regard to a whole series of great contemporary questions, for instance, the racial problem. All the churches which play an active part in the ecumenical movement have decided to support real justice in race relations. But a great deal still remains to be done before this consensus finds practical expression in the life of the local churches and of individual Christians, even in the countries which are not directly affected. But the main policy is clear.

All the churches in the ecumenical movement want to take part in the struggle for the recognition of human rights in legislation and in practice, including the right to religious liberty. We must hope that some of the less satisfactory sentences in the conciliar Decree, especially that on the special situation in countries with a very strong Catholic majority, will be interpreted *in bonam partem.*

All the churches in the ecumenical movement are discovering that the Church of Jesus Christ, which lives in all continents and directs its message of renewal to the whole of mankind, must play an outstanding part in the great effort to find a solution for the most burning problem of our time, namely the question how we can arrive on a world level at that minimum of social justice and equity without which peaceful coexistence is quite impossible.

Admittedly there are some extremely important questions on which the churches have not yet been able to reach a consensus. There is the tremendous menace of nuclear weapons. We are doing out utmost to achieve measures for nuclear disarmament, but we have no clear answer to the question whether all forms of nuclear armament should be condemned in themselves in the present situation. Unfortunately, we are not all in agreement about the very serious question of birth-control. The great majority of the churches belonging to the World Council of Churches are convinced that birth-control is essential in order to combat hunger and poverty, and that the methods medically approved should be accessible to everyone. The Catholic Church takes a different attitude; it only accepts the methods which it describes as "natural." I hope that we shall succeed in reaching a consensus on this difficult problem.

The methods which the churches should adopt also present a problem. In the international sphere the Catholic Church acts primarily through its diplomatic corps. The other churches do not think they ought to act in this way, because in their view church action should not be mixed with political action. It is interesting to note that the question was raised at the Vatican Council. In his speech Bishop Amman asked whether the appointment of diplomatic representatives did not give the impression that the Church resembles the powers of this world, thus concealing the real face of the Church. Several other Catholics, including several professors from the University of Nimwegen, have recently raised the same question. I venture to express the hope that this question will be subjected to very careful study, for it seems to me that joint action by the churches will be more effective if it adopts forms and methods which express the specifically spiritual character of the Church's presence in the world.

These divergences and difficulties must not prevent us from acting together in all questions where cooperation is already possible in all good faith. For instance there is the huge field

192

of work for refugees. There are common positions to be defended in the organs of the United Nations. And I hope the day will soon arrive when we shall be able to reach a consensus about the great international questions and crises (after previous consultation, of course) and about the way in which we should communicate our message to the world.

Is it not clear that in our divided world the Christian churches must do their utmost to make a united witness, the very existence of which shows that the people of God is a people reconciled by that same Lord, who can give the world the message of reconciliation for which it longs?

What have we to say about the new tasks of the churches in their relations to one another? In developing these relations I think a distinction can be drawn between three stages or periods. I would describe them as the stage of discovery, the stage of living together, and the stage of decision.

Before the ecumenical movement began, every church said, "As long as the other churches do not accept the Christian truth which has been revealed to me, I can have no contact with them." The ecumenical hour struck, and the first stage began, when the churches said, "There is a People of God, there are disciples of Jesus Christ, outside the life of my own institution. These other Christians are living in communities which, even if I cannot recognize them as churches in the full sense of the word, nor approve all that they teach, have clearly been used as vehicles by the Holy Spirit. I must therefore enter into fraternal relations with these churches, enter into conversation with them, and discover to what extent we can make a joint witness and collaborate together."

The first outcome of these contacts very often is that one dis-

193

covers with astonishment and gratitude that one shares many more convictions than one had thought. One even finds that these other churches have received spiritual gifts which are not as clearly apparent in one's own church. The tragedy of Christian division is not only that those who ought to live as a single reconciled people are divided by schisms, but also that these schisms prevent them from manifesting the wealth of harmony in the charismata which God has given to His Church. We must therefore learn to live together. We must emerge from our isolation and share our lives, or still better live for each other. That is the second stage. We can help each other; the churches are the protectors of their sister churches. The churches must exercise spiritual care over one another. That does not mean that there will be no more controversy; but it means that there will be mutual correction instead of destructive polemics. And that means that efforts will be made to cooperate wherever it is possible to do so with a good conscience.

That is already a great deal. But it is still not enough. For it is not sufficient for the churches to live side by side. They are called to manifest the unity of the People of God. That does not mean uniformity, but it does mean, the disappearance of all obstacles to real sacramental communion, and a common acceptance of structures which permit them to share their life, and to participate in joint witness and joint action.

In this third phase of ecumenical experience the churches must therefore ask themselves whether they are going to stop half-way, or whether they are going on to the end, whether unity is a lovely dream or whether it is really God's will for His people. This third period may therefore be called the period of ecumenical decision.

194

It seems to me that for many Churches, especially those which have been participating in the ecumenical movement for a long time, the question today is whether it is not their duty now to pass on from the second stage to the third. They have come to know one another. They have learned to live together in the World Council and in other bodies. That is already a great deal, but it is not enough. They must go on now until they have attained that true unity which will manifest that they all belong to the same Lord. It is a difficult moment, because it is also the moment when sacrifices have to be made. During the last few years we have seen that in such situations all sorts of non-theological factors are beginning to present obstacles to union.

In order to overcome all these obstacles we need to have a clear, strong conviction that unity is the will of God, and that this unity must be concrete, tangible, and visible. Many churches have realized this and have begun the slow, delicate task of seeking union with other churches. It is curious to note that in this respect the continent of Europe is the least active. It is like an underdeveloped continent in this respect. What are we waiting for to follow the example of all those churches in Asia, Africa, North America, and Great Britain which are making a genuine effort to arrive at union?

In the relations between the Roman Catholic Church and the other churches we are still in the *first* period, the period of discovery in which we are learning (after long years of isolation and estrangement) really to know each other, to explore the spiritual gifts of the other churches, to examine seriously the questions which they ask us. We have so much to learn. In this field we are all beginners. The Vatican Council was not only a school for the Catholic Bishops and for the members of the Catholic Church by opening up new horizons to them. We have all learned things that we never expected; we have all had to revise our previous opinions. But what has been said by authoritative voices in the Catholic Church is equally true, namely, that the existence and the experience of the ecumenical movement of the non-Catholic churches has been a real factor in the work of the Vatican Council.

The great question now is whether we shall really learn to live together with a sense of mutual responsibility and solidarity in a common vocation. There are encouraging signs. The dialogue has begun, not only on the level of the Churches but also on the local level. In many spheres—work among the laity and among young people, mission work, and of course in the field of theological study—the genuine exchange is increasing more and more. But obstacles still persist. The new ecumenical attitude has not yet permeated the whole life of our churches. The Catholics certainly still find many anti-Catholic reactions in the Protestant and Orthodox churches. And we, for our part, feel that there is a serious contradiction between the current practice concerning mixed marriages and the texts of the *Decree on Ecumenism* and the *Declaration on Religious Liberty*. We must therefore hope that on both sides we shall do our utmost to adjust the whole of our church life to the new situation. Many Catholics and many members of other churches, especially young people, have already gone beyond the first stage of discovery and have learned to live together in a real spiritual solidarity. Our Churches must attain the same solidarity.

Mention must also be made briefly of the new tasks on the parish level. The two essential things seem to me to be the following.

In the first place, we must help the members of our churches to think out their view of the Church entirely afresh. What I have in mind is not a revolution in the official ecclesiology of our churches. I am thinking of the real picture that our church members have of what the Church is. For I have the impression that in all our churches we are suffering from the same heresy—the idea that the Church belongs to men. We say *my* church, *our* church. We ask our churches to meet our wishes. We all need to be converted to the biblical idea that the Church is the People of God, the Body of Jesus Christ. It is only after this conversion that we shall be able to understand the spiritual need for unity. If the Church belongs to men, there is no reason why there should not be just as many churches as there are sports associations. But if the Church is in this world as a people set apart by God in order to preach and to manifest the great reconciliation in Christ, it is intolerable that there should be churches which are not really united among themselves.

The second thing to be done is to give everyone the opportunity for a genuine ecumenical experience. Teaching about ecumenical questions remains abstract and ineffective unless it is accompanied by real spiritual encounter with Christians of other churches. I have often found that ecumenical life begins at the moment when a member of a church recognizes a member of another church as a real servant of Jesus Christ. The ecumenical dialogue must therefore be opened on every level. This does not mean that everyone will participate in the discussion about doctrinal problems. Contacts between church members will rather take the form of a very simple exchange in which each has an opportunity to say what Christ means to him, what his church gives him and also of course an opportunity to make joint intercession for unity.

Praying together for unity means already receiving the first-fruits of unity. If I am separated from my brother who belongs to another church, I am also united with him in this intercession for unity. For we are submitting ourselves together to the Lord who is gathering us together, and who will keep his promise that there shall be one flock.

IX.

The Secretariat's Prospects
for the Reunification of Christians

BY AUGUSTIN CARDINAL BEA

Question: Should we not adhere to the idea that ecumenism, by virtue of its very spiritual and ecclesiastical dimensions, ought not to form a special sector reserved exclusively for the Secretariat, but rather that it should be seen as a component part of the entire realm of Church activity?

Answer: It would be good to bear in mind that the *Decree on Ecumenism* solemnly declares that the problem of re-establishing unity concerns the entire Church, laymen and clergy alike, each according to his ability. Of course the apostles' successors are primarily responsible for it. Ecumenism consti-tutes an important part of their activity as shepherds. The first problem which poses itself therefore involves coördination of this task which devolves upon the bishops. They must take the diversity of this situation into account, and avoid unnecessary centralization. As far as coordination of the Church's central direction is concerned, that is, among the curial authorities, this is to be carried out in accordance with the various usages by which the Church's many activities in the realm of spiritual welfare have been practised thus far, and which now, of course, have been set down within the framework of the curial reforms which were planned in compliance with modern criteria.

Question: As a consequence of its numerous and varied contacts with the World Council of Churches in Geneva, does the Secretariat intend to branch out into areas corresponding to those worked in by the World Council, or does it intend to be more of a coordinating center for all ecumenical aspects of the Church's many fields of activity, a center which is occasionally served by experts who do not normally belong to the Secretariat?

Answer: Let us not attempt to anticipate the future too much. Experience will show what is practical and what corresponds best to the Secretariat's concrete tasks. We must bear in mind that the Secretariat already has two sections, one for the Christian Orient and the other for reformatory Christians, with undersecretaries at their head. We must also consider the undeniable differences existing between the Secretariat's activity and that of the World Council of Churches. The Secretariat's activity is based on two main points of views: the first concerns the direction or coordination of ecumenical work within the Catholic Church itself, and the other involves contacts and cooperation with other Churches and/or communities and international organizations, respectively.

Question: Relations between Christian churches develop on two levels: on the one hand between Rome and the individual church in question, such as, for example, the Patriarchate of Constantinople—or, on the other hand, between totalities such as Rome and the World Council of Churches in Geneva. Could not this diversity of relationships be a cause for tensions? What could one do to promote mutual harmony and accord?

Answer: I spoke on this issue in the welcoming speech I delivered when visiting the main offices of the World Council of Churches last February 18th. At the time I said: "Just as, within the World Council of Churches, contacts exist, on the one hand, among various churches who are members of the World Council, and, on the other hand, among the member churches and the World Council itself, the Secretariat for Promoting Christian Unity (and through this Secretariat the Holy See itself) has made contacts with the individual churches and federations just as it has with the World Council itself, and it wishes to develop these contacts further. Just as I do not feel that this branching off into two directions might result in the creation of tensions between the World Council of Churches and its member organizations, I also do not see how such tensions could come about in the Council's contacts with the Secretariat. But should tensions arise now and then, we can always have recourse to a dialogue conducted in a fraternal spirit, so that all of our problems may be resolved in the light of truth and love. One example of how we can make progress in this area has been provided by the Central Committee of the World Council of Churches, and approved by the Holy See: we should explore hand in hand where and how we can begin cooperating and conducting our dialogue starting now, while awaiting any other ways and opportunities which might present themselves as time goes on. In other words, in this instance we should not lay out any definite plan. We must make headway in a concrete manner, as I explained during my conversation last February with Dr. Boegner in Geneva, that is to say, we must consider each case according to its own merits and according to the prevailing circumstances, with sincerity and docility towards the Holy Spirit who guides us all in accordance with the mysterious designs of his wisdom and love.

201

Question: We would like to pose one last question to Your Eminence. Consideration has been given to the creation of a mixed study group composed of representatives from the Roman Church and the Patriarchate of Constantinople. What would be the relationship of this group to the mixed commission formed by members of the World Council and the Secretariat for Promoting Christian Unity?

Answer: A group such as this is actually being considered. It would mainly have to conduct a pastoral dialogue and view the bearing of its responsibility towards modern men as a common Church task. With reference to relationships between this group and the mixed commission formed by members of the World Council of Churches and the Catholic Church, we can say nothing at this time. We must first of all see what results and conclusions are obtained from the one as well as the other study group. We could perhaps, in conclusion, point out one last thought which, in a certain sense, might prevail over all of these replies. It is the thought which I formulated as follows in the speech delivered in Geneva, to which I have already made reference: "Above all else I would like to guard against the misunderstanding that this question might be dealt with on the basis of previously established patterns. No such schemata exist, nor could they exist, just as there are no schemata for a dialogue between individuals. Instead, we must look at the actual situation of the person or persons who are to participate in such a dialogue in order to decide, step by step, what must be done and what course should be taken." The same also applies to further development of the Secretariat's work.

In this connection it would be appropriate to call to mind the words with which the Holy Father addressed the observer delegates at the September 29, 1964, audience: "You can see how prepared the Catholic Church is for an honorable and sincere dialogue. There is no rush, yet it ardently desires for this dialogue to begin, and entrusts its completion to the grace of God, however and whenever it shall be deemed appropriate."

However, I can and must add just one more thought. All of this effort towards slowly and patiently investigating ways and means of rapprochement must be governed by an enduring awareness of the fact that we are not the ones who are the guiding influence. The Holy Spirit is the guiding force. It is for us to carry out his spirit. For those who are led by the spirit of God are his sons (Rom. 8, 14). We must therefore follow the inspiration of the Holy Spirit with humility and docility, with the magnanimity of love, and with full awareness that "God is at work in you, both to will and to work for his good pleasure" (Phil. 2, 13).

This last thought reminds me of what Pope Paul VI said at the aforementioned audience concerning the results achieved thus far: "The fact that mutual satisfaction with our many meetings is far from diminishing and far from proving to be a disappointment, but that, to the contrary, it is in part becoming more active and worthy of trust at this time constitutes an excellent result, so we feel. It is a historical fact that our true and complete unity in Jesus Christ, which is the highest possible goal towards which we must strive in concerted effort, must be evaluated positively. Any possible abyss of distrusting and skepticism has been overcome for the most part. Your very presence here indicated and promotes the type of spiritual rapprochement with which we were not familiar thus far. A new method has revealed itself to us, friendship has been born, hope has been aroused, a movement has begun. Praise to God who, we do believe, has given his Holy Spirit unto us (1 Thess. 4, 8)."

X.

Pluralism—Temptation or Opportunity

BY WILLEM A. VISSER 'T HOOFT

I SHALL ATTEMPT to discuss the question of pluralism in its world setting and from the point of view of the ecumenical movement.

There are many definitions of pluralism. For our purpose it is sufficient to say that the word describes a situation in which various religious, philosophical, or ideological conceptions live side by side and in which none of them holds a privileged status.

Our world has always been pluralistic in the sense that there have always been a great variety of religions, of philosophies and conceptions of life. But until the time of the Reformation, and in many countries until our own time, religious plurality was not a fact of experience. The churches lived in self-contained communities. *Cuius regio, eius religio* remained the dominating principle for a long time. And even when it proved necessary to arrive at adjustments between different Christian confessions, the pluralism was only a pluralism within a common Christian tradition. Thus the country which, for obvious reasons, pioneered in the working out of the pluralistic principle, namely the United States, continued to attach strong importance to its definitely Christian tradition. It is only in our days that the churches have come to face the issue of pluralism in its sharper form, namely, as the appearance on their own doorstep of a multitude of other conceptions of life, religious positions, or ideologies which claim the same rights as the Churches. It would seem that the main factors in the creation of modern pluralism are the following five:

The first factor is the continuing process of secularization. The original meaning of the term is that properties or institutions which belonged to the Church passed into the hands of government or non-ecclesiastical bodies in general. Later on it took on the meaning of the cessation of the monopolistic position of the Church in the field of education and culture and of the emergence of various social and cultural forces as independent sources of creative participation in the life of society. And more recently it is used to indicate a process of emancipation of life from any religious authority or standard.

We must distinguish between the process of secularization and the philosophy of secularism. Secularization does not necessarily lead to secularism. It leads most often to pluralism. As the ecclesiastical control weakens, a great many different centers of energy begin to operate. Some of these are religious, some of them non-religious. At the same time the traditional churches continue to exist and often show a surprising tenacity and power of adaptation. The late 19th-century prophecies that the Roman Catholic Church was a dying Church; the Marxist prophecies concerning the inevitable disappearance of religion in communist societies; the national socialist hopes that the churches could be eliminated, have all proved completely false. In fact, the secularization process has often meant that the Church found new freedom and new vigor. In other words, secularization means that there is now a firm foundation for endeavor to

206

new polarization of fundamental convictions and a baffling variety of choices.

The second factor is closely connected with the first. It is the world-wide movement for the recognition and promotion of human rights and particularly of the rights of freedom of conscience, freedom of association, and freedom to advocate religious and philosophical convictions. In a certain sense religious liberty is the product of pluralism. For it is when the complete overlapping of membership in the national church ceases to be self-evident and when dissenting and non-conformist convictions become sufficiently strong, that religious freedom becomes inevitable. So it was inevitable that the churches coming out of a great variety of religious, ideological, and cultural situations to form the ecumenical movement should take the issue of religious liberty immediately. So they did at Amsterdam, Evanston, and New Delhi.

Similarly, the Vatican Council declaration recognized that:

In view of the increasing international relations between people of different cultures and religions and for the establishment and strengthening of peaceful relations and concord in the human family, it is necessary that throughout the world religious liberty should be provided with effective legal safeguards and that the supreme duty and right of man freely to lead a religious life in society should be observed.

On the other hand, religious freedom gives a strong, new impetus to pluralism, because it makes the expression of minority views less costly and so encourages their manifestation. In our time, the freedom of conscience and the expression of religious, philosophical, or ideological convictions has at last become an almost universally accepted norm of society. That does not mean that it is universally practiced. In large areas of the world these basic human rights are in fact neglected or even denied. But it is nevertheless important that the principle has been established through the Universal Declaration of Human Rights and corresponding statements in many national constitutions, for this means that there is now a firm foundation for endeavors to make religious freedom effective. The fact that the Roman Catholic Church, which had been so reluctant to accept this human right, has now also recognized it, is not only important because this will make the situation for non-Catholic minorities in some strongly Roman Catholic countries a good deal easier, but also and especially because it means that the Roman Catholic Church joins the ranks of supporters of the most fundamental of all human rights.

There is another sense in which religious freedom leads to greater pluralism. When religious freedom is granted, the question arises sooner or later whether those individuals or groups which hold non-religious and anti-religious positions should not have the same rights as those who advocate a religious conception of life. In many traditionally Christian countries this is now a deeply controversial question. Shall humanists and atheists have the same rights in broadcasting, in the field of education, in relation to the armed forces as those that have been given to the churches? Must religious pluralism lead to a wider pluralism in which every conception or philosophy of life has equal opportunity?

The third factor is the reactivation of national cultures which has gone on together with the emergence of many formerly dependent nations as active participants in the world community. For it is natural that these cultures emphasize their specific heritage. Each heritage has its religious roots. So the national revival leads to a rediscovery of ancient religious traditions, though these traditions may be reëvaluated and reinterpreted in order to make them effective in the new situation. It is impossible to predict what the results of this process will be, whether it will lead to a genuine renaissance of Hinduism, of Buddhism, of Islam; or whether the nationalistic component will be so powerful that the religious component will suffer and, slowly but surely, be overcome by various forms of secularism. But it is clear that for many years to come the main historic religions will be powerful factors in the world scene, that all of them are developing increasingly a consciousness of worldwide missionary responsibility; and that, just as Christianity has penetrated into their territory, so they will penetrate into territories which have been traditionally Christian.

The fourth factor is the external unification of the world. Can unification then produce pluralism? It can, if it is a unification in the means of communication rather than in the content of ultimate convictions. And that is precisely what has happened. It is through the migration and travels of persons and the intensive interchange of ideas that religious and ideological influences which had so far been imprisoned within definite geographical boundaries, now play their world-wide role. The old maps, which divided the world so neatly in regions with different colors for each religion, are becoming out of date. These maps with black for the "pagans," yellow for the Moslems, red for the Roman Catholics, and green (explained as the color of hope) for the Protestants would now have to look like an abstract painting seeking to put the maximum number of colors in the minimum amount of space. It is true that, even today, more or less official statistics are published according to which about 90 per cent of the inhabitants of France are Roman Catholics or more than 90 per cent of the inhabitants of Sweden are Protestants. But no one who has ever taken note of the findings of the sociology of religions can take such figures seriously. In a certain sense such statistics underline the pluralistic character of our modern society. For if the Roman Catholic Church in Italy claims that more than 50 million of 51 million Italians belong to it and the communist party in the same country is the largest communist party outside the communist controlled world, this can only mean that, for a large number of Italians, pluralism is not only a problem of relationships with others, but a conflict within their own personal lives.

But there is last, not least, a fifth factor. Pluralism is not only the result of developments in the life of the world. It is not only imposed on the churches. The churches themselves have strongly contributed to its rise.

The old monolithic societies, the *Corpora Christiana,* in which church, state, and community were inseparable and overlapping were, in fact, maintaining the church in a tight embrace in which it could not breathe and act freely. Thus the movements of renewal in the church—whether of more pietistic or of more ecclesiocentric origin—all tended to give to the church again its own distinct function and place. Free churches arose and fought for equal rights with the established churches. But once this right was granted the way to the wider pluralism had been opened.

Thus the churches find themselves in a new situation. No church can claim any more that it alone represents the convictions and aspirations of a whole people. And even the claim that the Christian churches together are an adequate reflection of the deeper convictions of the community as a whole has become untenable in most so-called Christian countries. And when the churches look out upon the world situation they do not see what our fathers saw at the beginning of the century— namely, a world which is on the way to becoming Christianized, but rather a world in which the non-Christian religious and ideological forces make more rapid advance than Christianity.

The picture that we see today is one where only a small part of the world is under the influence of Christian governments (and, let it be added, governments which are often more eager to demonstrate their perfect religious neutrality than any interest in the Christian cause), where an enormous part of the world is under the influence of Marxism, and where in many other countries Christian missions are practically unable to operate.

Do the churches realize the full significance of the new pluralism? I doubt it. Their reaction is often a reaction of bewilderment, sometimes even of panic.

The main reason why the churches are reluctant to face up to the fact of pluralism is that they find it so hard to give up the ideal of an integrated Christian society inspired by one particular church or by all the churches together. Now this is to their credit insofar as it means that they refuse to give up their claim that the Christian Gospel is fundamentally universal in its scope, addressed to all men and meant to penetrate all areas of society. But it is one thing to stand for the unlimited lordship of Christ; it is another to speak and act as if the general recognition and acceptance of the lordship can be expected to take place in the near future. In this regard it is interesting to note that in the early days of the ecumenical movement the ideal of "the Christian society" still played a great role. The COPEC meeting of the British churches in 1924 stated that it is in the medieval idea of the *Respublica Christiana*—a single, universal community, founded and governed by God Himself, that the authentic message of Christianity is to be looked for, at least potentially.[1] And the report of the British section to the Stockholm Life and Work Conference of 1925 called the League of Nations Covenant a beginning from which the world-wide Christian commonwealth might gradually be built up, a commonwealth based on a common faith which would give birth to a common culture. Similar ideas came at that time from Social Gospel theologians in the United States and France.

By the time of the Oxford Conference on Church, Community, and State in 1937, the climate had changed. Instead of being on the way towards a new Christian integration, the world seemed to fall into the hands of pagan ideological forces. With regard to the old Christendom concept the conference spoke a sober and realistic word: 'Today convinced Christians are everywhere in a minority in a predominantly unchristian world . . . The church has not yet faced the new situation with sufficient frankness. With the conservative instincts of all institutions of long standing and influence it has fought a defensive —and on the whole a losing—battle for the maintenance of as much as possible of the old ideal of the *Corpus Christianum* and of the privileges and authority which that implies. But such a policy is doubly mistaken. First it is quite unrealistic. The younger churches have never wielded such an authority, and for the older churches it is irrevocably gone, at least for the present

1. COPEC Report on International Relations, pp. 119–120.

era. Secondly, the ideal itself, though magnificent, was mistaken and premature. In practice it entailed more accommodation of the church to the world than of the world to the church."[2]

If these words had been taken seriously by all churches they would now be in a better position to face the present world; they would have lost less time and energy in defending "privileges and authority" which are by no means essential for the fulfillment of their central task; they would take up their new tasks in a pluralistic world with more confidence.

But what is the task of the church in the pluralistic world-society?

Let us first deal with the temptations which the church must resist and then discuss what opportunity is offered to it.

1. The Temptation of the Return to Christendom

The first temptation is surely to believe, in spite of the evidence, that it is possible to return to the situation of the past.

Are then all defenders of the idea of an integrated Christian society like the Danish king who, the story goes, commanded the waves to recede? Some of them are, indeed. They dream of a restoration of the old monolithic world of Christendom in which the Church could easily deal with any competitors which appeared on the scene and in which pluralism was not a problem because, as a well-known historian put it, those who did not accept the official faith were occupied with being burned.

In the great debate about religious liberty before and during the Second Vatican Council a main argument of the opposition

2. *The Churches Survey their Task,* pp. 200–201.

was that the granting of religious liberty meant the giving up of the great ideal which had been so staunchly defended by many popes: the ideal of a fully integrated Christian society in which all would be expected to regulate their lives by the teachings of the one Church and in which dissenters could at best be tolerated on the condition that they would keep quiet. Thus Bishop Del Campo said that with the present new declaration, a centuries-old religious patrimony was endangered, and that the sociological fact of pluralism could not modify and correct the doctrinal principles of the Church. And Cardinal De Arriba y Castro of Spain warned the Council in September, 1956, not to adopt a decree which would spell the ruin of Catholicism in nations where it is in fact the only religion. According to him, non-Catholic bodies should only have the right to meet privately.

The voting on the *Declaration on Religious Liberty* has shown that the defenders of the traditional *Corpus Christianum* conception are now a minority in the Roman Catholic Church. It is one of the most remarkable aspects of the great change in the attitude of Roman Catholics to the world that the nostalgia for the medieval unitary society which was so prominent in Roman Catholic thought until recently, has ceased to play a dominating role. Up to the time of Pope John XXIII the popes in speaking about international relations again and again presented the "Christendom" structure of the Middle Ages as the ideal pattern of international life. It is significant that Pope Paul VI did not do so when he spoke to the United Nations.

There are, however, voices which cannot possibly be dismissed as voices of reaction and which advocate the idea of a Christian society in a new form. They are so deeply impressed by the continuing process of the disintegration of the spiritual, moral, and

214

cultural fabric of modern society and they are so certain that no society can live without a religious basis, that they seek desperately for new ways of christianizing the common life.

One such recently is Père Jean Daniélou, in his *L'Oraison, problème politique.* He has given a lively apologia for the concept of Christendom. He argues that Constantine is not, as so many think, the villain of the piece. On the contrary, we owe it to Constantine that Christianity became the religion of the people rather than of a spiritual élite. Ordinary people cannot live the Christian life unless they are supported by a Christianized society. "Il n'y a pas de christianisme de masse sans chrétienté."[1]

The Church must not consider other religions or the various forms of natural religion as its enemies. Bonhoeffer and his followers are wrong in thinking that revelation can live without religion. We need a new Christian civilization, and it is perfectly possible to pass from a traditional type of Christian society to a renewed Christian society without passing through the stage of dechristianization.

I have considerable sympathy with the concern that lies behind these attempts to present the ideal of a unified and coherent culture in a new form. If one sees the speed and extent of the disintegration of national cultures, the difficulty of governing peoples which have no longer a common ethos, the sterility which threatens artistic creation when it is no longer rooted in a coherent society, one is forced to look for a new force of integration. But we must not take our desires for realities. And it seems to me that this is what both T. S. Eliot and thinkers like Père Daniélou have done. Their construction has three points of weakness.

1. Page 15.

The first with regard to diagnosis. They do not seem to take fully seriously that such a very large part of the population in most parts of the world has lost any real contact with Christianity. This becomes especially clear in Père Daniélou's remarks about modern atheism. He tells us several times[1] that "atheism is an accident" or "a moment of crisis," so that it is wrong to think that it is the problem of tomorrow.

Now I would agree that in their diagnosis of the trends of the time, some of our modern prophets are too exclusively pre-occupied with the phenomenon of non-religious men who *feel* that God is dead—and do not mind. There is at the same time the emergence of many new forms of religiosity and syncretism. But to speak and act as if atheism need not concern us in our thinking about the future of the Church is an extraordinary over-simplification. Any study of the results of religious sociology should convince us that in most countries we are in the position that at present and for a long time to come we will not be able to build a Christian society for the simple reason that there are not enough Christians left who can form such a society. And this leads to the second reason.

The only real Christendom that has ever existed was based on compulsion. If we want to "reinstate religion as the central integrating force in society" we are really talking about "something which has never yet been done on the large scale of modern society, and to do it under conditions of intellectual and political freedom."[2] So the defenders of the idea of the Christian society should tell us whether they really want the state to act as *de-*

1. Pages 70, 99, and 128.
2. H. Paul Douglass, in *Church and Community*. Oxford Conference, Volume, p. 251.

fensor fidei, the very idea which practically all churches, including the Roman Catholic Church have now given up—or whether they have found another method of transforming within the foreseeable future a pluralist society into an integrated *Corpus Christianum.*

The third weakness of their position is that they do not ask whether a restoration of the Christian society is compatible with the insight that has been given to our generation concerning the real nature of the Church. In the Christendom situation, "The Church," says Sir Ernest Barker, "ceased to be a pure body bearing the custody of the Word and knit organically to its Head; it became the alter ego of another body, subject to the fortunes and the historic vicissitudes of that other body."[1] But the costly lessons which the churches have had to learn in our time all point in the same direction: "Let the Church be the Church," let it be bound to its Lord and free from outside control, let it be in the world but not of the world. And a church which takes that insight about its own life and mission seriously cannot accept to enter once again into that most entangling of alliances on which any concrete elaboration of a specifically Christian society is based.

2. *The Temptation of Introversion*

To live in the midst of a pluralistic world, to maintain one's spiritual integrity in that world and yet to be fully involved in its ideological conflicts, in its moral dilemmas, in its search for a better world is a hard task. It is therefore not difficult to under-

1. *Church and Community,* page 46.

stand that many Christians turn away from that world. Is not the new pluralism further proof that this world belongs to the Prince of this world, the diabolos that is the creator of confusion and chaos? And has not the Kingdom of God been promised to the little flock which is not of this world? As they see how the traditional structures of the Christian society collapse and the old moral standards lose their authority, they withdraw into their small groups and develop the psychology of the besieged fortress. Many, who discover that we are no longer living in the days when Christian missions could tell an exciting success-story, begin to lose interest in the missionary task of the church. Many, seeing that the old international supremacy of the Christian powers has disappeared and that it is utopian to expect that in the foreseeable future the international order shall be Christianized, give up any effort to exert Christian influence in the field of international affairs. But in doing so they give up at the same time two convictions which are indispensable ingredients of the Christian faith. The first is that the good news concerning God's intervention in the life of humanity through Jesus Christ is to be proclaimed to all. This truth is not merely valid for times when there are open doors on all sides. It is just as valid when Christianity has to go against what seems the main current of history. Christians who let their zeal for evangelism depend on tangible, visible, and immediate results have lost their sense of the specific quality of the divine as contrasted with our human history. Missions today are again the test of the reality of our faith in the universal dimension of the Gospel and in the divine promise which is connected with it.

In the second place, an introverted Christianity denies the prophetic ministry to which the church and its members are called. For a long time the churches had forgotten that part of their calling. And even today they exercise it hesitantly and intermittently. But we know at least that it belongs to real Christian obedience. And we know that the prophet cannot be an opportunist in the ordinary sense of that word, because he is made aware of an opportunity created by God who overrules the calculations of men. Here again success or failure are not decisive categories. Nor need a church be influential or powerful to speak the liberating word to the people.

To accept that the church should just live its introverted life within its own walls is to accept and confirm the false view of the church which is held by those, whether of the communist or capitalist persuasion who have absolutized their economic and social philosophies and consider that the church should never express any judgment on social or political affairs except insofar as it gives spiritual support to the official position. That attitude remains amazingly persistent. If we just take the examples of recent months we find that the German church leaders are sharply criticized for having taken a stand on the question of the German territories which now form part of Poland, that the British churches are under similar criticism for their stand concerning South Africa and Rhodesia, that South African Christians who question the doctrine of apartheid are treated as traitors to their country. In the United States the criticism against the churches for their concern about civil rights is still widespread.

3. The Temptation of Relativism

It is natural that for many people the logical conclusion to be drawn from the pluralistic state of our society is that the very notion of unique truth should be abandoned. For them pluralism as a description of a factual situation leads in a straight line to pluralism as a philosophy of life. It is probably no accident that it was in the United States, almost the only nation which has had pluralism in its bones since its very birth, that the name pluralism was first given to a system of philosophy. This was done by William James in his book on *The Pluralistic Universe*. James challenged all forms of monism. "He was not interested in the One, but in the many." Professor Patrick[1] in describing this philosophy quotes Robert Louis Stevenson:

> The world is so full of a number of things
> I am sure we should all be as happy as kings.

That was written in the time when pluralism seemed to offer a way of escape from the monistic philosophies and from a rather uniform cultural pattern.

In the meantime we have learned to think more soberly about pluralism. We see its necessity, but we realize also that it has its specific dangers and especially we recognize that ideological diversity may lead to cold or even total warfare. So we are more inclined to think of pluralism as an inevitable fact of modern life than as a cure for all ills.

The relativist argues that pluralism is the natural result of religious liberty and that religious liberty presupposes the recognition that no one has the whole truth and that there is some truth in every religious or philosophical tradition.

If pluralism would really mean that in matters of religion and philosophy of life everybody is more or less right except those who believe that they have found truth which has its own objective validity independent of its recognition, and that therefore no one should seek to persuade his fellow men to accept another

1. *The World and its Meaning,* p. 257.

conviction than the one he holds already, then all Christians should have to fight pluralism as an invention of the devil. For it would then breed a race of spiritually spineless human beings who would live in the sort of night in which all cats are grey. No one would any longer have to face the ultimate questions of life. One would not have to answer the questions of Jesus: "Who do you think I am?" and "Will you follow me?" It would be a terribly dull world in which one would begin to long again for a serious spiritual conflict. Fortunately we do not live in that world. We live in a world where the man who wants to live responsibly must choose, whether he likes it or not.

In this connection it is interesting to note that the final text of the *Declaration on Religious Liberty* of the Second Vatican Council contains, on the one hand, clear statements concerning the right of every person to enjoy religious liberty but, on the other hand, a most emphatic affirmation that the only true religion is to be found in the Catholic and apostolic Church. Many eyebrows were raised when this last affirmation was introduced in the last drafts. As a matter of fact it did not have much influence on the attitude of the opposition for the number of negative votes remained unchanged. My own feeling is that while the wording of this conviction is unfortunate in that it does not include the qualifications made in the *Decree on Ecumenism,* it is nevertheless useful to show that it is possible to accept pluralism as the pattern of modern society without embracing a religious or doctrinal relativism.

We cannot help trying to persuade each other. Even our relativists seek to convert us all. So let us agree that pluralism must mean a truly open situation in which all have the right to persuade all and in which we respect in each other the seriousness

221

and sincerity with which convictions are held and expressed. A Marxist professor from Prague said recently in a discussion in Germany: "I take only such Christians seriously who try to convert me."[1] This Marxist has a deeper understanding of the nature of truth than many Christians for whom their faith is just one of the many possible ways to find meaning in life.

It is strange, and at the same time revealing, that at a time when in the realm of religion the sense of the absolute weakens, absolutism grows in political life. Does this not mean that man cannot live in a world where there is no center and no guiding star and that, if no trustworthy truth is offered to him in the right place he will look for it in the wrong place?

4. The Temptation of Syncretism

The nostalgia for the past, the withdrawal from the spiritual and ideological battle, the transformation of pluralistic facts into pluralistic norms—none of these attitudes come to grips with the seriousness and the magnitude of the problem. For if they continue to give different and contradictory answers to the basic questions of the meaning of life and the true standards of human conduct, there remain the haunting questions how men can live together in the small world of our time and how they can find common solutions for their common problems so as to avoid destroying each other in their ideological conflicts. Is there any chance for the establishment of order and justice on a global scale unless we can get the whole of humanity to accept a body of laws and rights and ensure that these laws be maintained and these rights respected? And can there be any system of law with-

1. *Evang. Pressedienst,* 12 October 1965.

222

out some common ethos, some general recognition of a body of moral values? And again, can there be a common ethos without a basic agreement about the ultimate issues of truth? Are we not therefore driven to demand that the present pluralistic pattern be overcome as soon as possible and that a world religion be established? And since there is not the slightest chance in the present circumstances that one of the existing religions or philosophies will be accepted by all as the one normative world-faith for the world-community, are we not forced to the conclusion that we must synthesize the existing religions and ideologies and thus create a genuine world-faith? Or to put the matter more shortly: Should true world-citizens today become syncretists?

These are questions which deserve to be taken seriously. The fact that many of the attempts to elaborate a universal synthesis are superficial and naïve does not necessarily mean that the concept of a world-religion is to be rejected. And we Christians, advocating Christianity, have so often used the argument that a world faith is absolutely indispensable for the life of humanity, that we have no right to laugh about people who use similar arguments, and who come, in the light of the present situation, to the conclusion that that world religion must be a mixture of Christianity and other religions.

Why, then, do I speak of syncretism as a temptation, as a misleading answer to the problem of pluralism? For three reasons.

The first is that any religion which contains a strong transcendent and prophetic element will defend its spiritual integrity against the attempt to use it for human purposes, however good these human purposes may be.

It is the very nature of prophetic religion to awaken men from

223

that sleepy and static condition in which they find themselves as long as their religion is merely a traditional cult maintained for the sake of social cohesion. To use religion in order to unify the world is really to return to the religious policies of some of the Roman emperors for whom religion was an instrument of imperial policy.

Already, in the days of the League of Nations, we often heard voices such as that of Alfred Loisy who said: "The League of Nations *demands* a religion of humanity."[1] And in our time, when catastrophe seems to be just around the corner and the United Nations is paralyzed by ideological conflict, that same demand is more insistent than ever. But real religion is not a commodity to be ordered. Will Herberg, in the fine concluding chapter of his *Protestant, Catholic and Jew,* has made the issue very clear. What he has to say about "the underlying culture-religion of America—best understood as the religious aspect of the American way of life" which is really religion used for material purposes and "a kind of protection the self throws up against the radical demand of faith," applies not only to the United States and to the present day. It is a very ancient, very persistent, and very general temptation. Now a world religion created in order to give the world community the necessary cohesion would have these same basically idolatrous characteristics together with the glamour of its universal claim. Soloviev saw this when in his famous apocalyptic vision he portrayed the Antichrist as the protagonist of a religion in which humanity adored itself.

The second reason is that a synthetic universal religion cannot be fabricated. It has been tried more than once.

New manufacturers of the universal religion arise in every

1. Quoted in *Universal Church and the World of Nations,* p. 41.

generation. Thus Professor Northrop of Yale, in *The Meeting of East and West* feels, like Akbar four centuries ago, that the social policies, moral ideals, and religious aspirations of men, because of their incompatability one with another will continue to generate misunderstanding and war "unless the ideological conflicts are faced and, if possible, resolved."[1] And he proceeds therefore to inquire whether a synthesis can be worked out. He takes the pieces of the gigantic puzzle and tries to fit them together. Does he succeed? He believes that a good many important pieces such as Western science, Eastern religion, certain forms of Catholicism (especially the cult of the Virgin in Mexico) and even democracy and communism can, after some adjustment, be made into one whole. Unfortunately other pieces of the puzzle—and notably the basic elements of the Hebrew-Christian tradition—somehow do not fit into the new pattern. So the synthesis is not so universal after all.

I do not want to be malicious. But these artificial constructions make me think of one of the worst meals I have ever had to swallow. It was arranged by a fanatic internationalist. He had invited some ten couples of ten different nationalities. Each was to bring a special national dish. You can imagine the result!

The third reason is that it is misleading to say that we must choose between continued conflict, leading to catastrophe, on the one hand, and the creation of one common world religion on the other. That kind of statement has been made thousands of times, by Christians when seeking to justify their missionary efforts, and by syncretists, when offering their recipe for a new synthesis. But repetition does not make it true. It is not impossible for men of differing religions and ideological persuasion to live together in such a way that they do not make life impossible for

1. P. ix.

each other. In a moment we will have to say more about the requirements of such living together in a pluralistic world. Now we note that pluralism, rightly understood, is not necessarily a cause of friction. We must not forget that the great temptation of an all-powerful religion is to suppress religious minorities and that numerous inter-religious conflicts have been caused precisely by the attempt to make one religion a world religion without competitors. The plurality of religions and ideologies brings with it infinite possibilities of misunderstanding and conflicts, but attempts to force the situation by the imposition of one religion or ideology make the situation worse.

We have tried to state how we should *not* react to the new pluralist situation. This was the easier part of our task. For it is much harder to give a satisfactory positive formulation of the Christian attitude in this matter. The difficulty is that the Christian church cannot possibly advocate pluralism as an ideal. Its raison d'être is to bring all men to Christ; its universalism implies the hope that pluralism will not have the last word. On the other hand we do not want to appear half-hearted in our acceptance of pluralism. The theory that pluralism is only a necessary evil to be tolerated as long as convinced and committed Christians are in a minority position, but that as soon as they can dominate the situation, they must seek to impose their standards and patterns, looks too much like the theory of the thesis and the hypothesis held by traditionalist Roman Catholic theologians, rejected by the advocates of genuine religious liberty and now happily abandoned in the new *Declaration on Religious Liberty* of the Second Vatican Council.

It is of course true that many churches have resisted the development of a pluralist society until they began to see that the monolithical concept of society could be used against them. Perhaps the most impressive plea for religious liberty in the Second Vatican Council was made by Cardinal Beran of Czechoslovakia who knew from bitter experience what could happen to the Church in an ideologically controlled nation. In the ecumenical movement the concern for religious liberty had its origin in missionary circles where it was realized that the doors were being closed for the missionary witness in many countries dominated by other religions. Are we therefore only accepting pluralism, because the shoe is now on the other foot and Christians can no longer have it their own way?

I believe that there is a better reason. It is that pluralism rightly understood creates for the church a situation in which it is less in danger of falsifying its own nature and in which it is better able to manifest its true calling. Pluralism provides the church with a God-given opportunity to live according to its own inherent spiritual law.

The pluralistic society gives the church a chance to be the church rather than what Sir Ernest Barker called "the alter ego of another body."[1] It takes away privileges which have often proved a spiritual handicap rather than a help to its work. It makes, as the Oxford Conference said, "membership in the church more costly and mere conformity less attractive."[2] And, what is most important, it forces the Church to render its witness in a manner consonant with the content of that witness.

There is a remarkable passage on this subject in the early Christian Epistle to Diognetus (chapter 7). It says: "Well, then,

1. *Church, Community and State,* p. 46.
2. *Report,* p. 201.

did God send him (Jesus) as any man might expect, to play the dictator and inspire fear and terror? By no means, but in humility (the same word as in the Beatitude concerning the humble) and magnanimity he sent him, as a king sending a royal son; as God he sent him, as a man to men he sent him, as saving he sent him, as persuading, not violently compelling, for violence belongeth not to God."

Now if, as the whole New Testament tells us, Jesus came as the *praus,* the humble and gentle who simply offered Himself and His Gospel without any attempt to force it upon men or to support it by anything that was not the Gospel itself, His church is in the right, the normal position, when, according to Pascal's expression, it is supported only by God. That is the situation into which the pluralist society puts the church. And therefore we have not only no reason to be afraid of it, but we can rejoice in it.

But we have yet to go a long way before our churches have learned their lessons and fully understood how to use the new opportunities offered to them. We must work out a new strategy for our action in the pluralist world. This implies, first of all, that we play an active role in the working out of what may be called the rules of spiritual traffic in a pluralist society; and, secondly, that we learn ourselves to observe these rules.

What are some of these rules? I would offer the following suggestions, which are not exhaustive.

In the first place, there must be liberty for all to express their convictions. That seems obvious. But in fact it is still widely held that there should be liberty for all religious positions, but not for non-religious or anti-religious philosophies of life. When, at the time of the Odessa meeting of the World Council of Churches,

Dr. Nolde stated this principle of liberty for all, many were deeply shocked that a Christian body could ask for freedom for atheists as well as for religious believers. At this point the Declaration of the Vatican is not definite. It could perhaps be deduced from the words: "Libertas in *re religiosa*"—but it is not explicitly stated. Is it not clear that our own demand for true spiritual freedom remains unconvincing unless we are willing to grant that freedom to all? It is precisely on the basis of the universal principle that we are then able to protest against any interference with spiritual liberty. Anti-religious propaganda is not really dangerous for the church. It often leads to clarification of the true nature of the Christian faith. Far more dangerous are the administrative measures which many communist and some other governments take against the church and against these we can only speak out (I say this on the basis of recent experience) if we appeal to the observance of the rules of the game as it ought to be played between fair-minded people.

In the second place, no group must ask for special privileges which it is not willing to give to others. It is important that the *Declaration on Religious Liberty* of the Second Vatican Council states that when, in special circumstances, a religious community enjoys special recognition by the state, it is necessary that at the same time religious liberty be granted to all citizens and to all religious communities. But the question arises whether such special recognition accorded to one community does not in fact mean that other bodies are handicapped from the outset. The sooner we arrive at true equality of opportunity for all spiritual and philosophical families, the better for the health of our mutual relationships.

In the third place, genuine pluralism requires that we resist policies destined to neutralize specific and definite convictions and to establish a uniform lowest common denominator of all philosophies and creeds. There are today many national and international institutions and foundations which are so afraid of what they call sectarianism that they avoid any dealings with or encouragement of churches or movements which have a clearly defined basis of conviction and seek to promote a so-called nonsectarian approach to all social, national, or international problems. But, in so doing, they are consciously or unconsciously promoting a secularistic type of uniformity which discriminates against all positive beliefs and is thus on the way to creating a spineless indifferentism.

In the fourth place, all must be willing to enter into dialogue with all and in this dialogue all must be willing to give an account of their convictions and allow their own convictions to be challenged by the convictions of others. Dialogue is only meaningful when all the cards are put on the table and no issue is considered too delicate or too difficult to be discussed. Now dialogue requires, of course, a certain open-mindedness. But open-mindedness is not everything. Dialogue between two minds which are open all the time and in all directions can hardly lead to a real "*choc des opinions*" which produces truth. I suppose that the death-certificate of the classical donkey which could not make up its mind whether to eat the hay on the left or the hay on the right, said something like: died from starvation caused by acute and persistent open-mindedness. Dialogue is spiritual battle for truth. It is battle not of the partners against each other, for neither can say that his position is simply to be identified with the truth. It is battle, in that both become involved in the conflict between truth and error and both want truth to win. But it is *spiritual* battle. None but spiritual weapons are allowed. There is place for persuasion, not for violence. Christians can learn from their New Testament that humility does not exclude assurance and firmness of faith and that the spiritual warfare, as described in Ephesians 5 is not destructive, but seeks to build up. The New English Bible translates Eph. 5, 17: "For sword, take that which the Spirit gives you, the words that come from God."

In the fifth place, we have to seek constantly for common objectives with all other groups in society, even with those whose fundamental positions are furthest removed from our own. Christians ought to be the first, not the last to come out of their isolation and try to find out how far they can go with others in working for such specific positive goals as the observance of human rights, the removal of the injustice of the discrepancy between living standards, the support of developing nations. Not to do so is to deny our faith in the solidarity of all men based on the fact that one died for all. It is possible for men who disagree deeply in their fundamental assumptions to agree on specific constructive tasks which must be accomplished for the good of all. That happens constantly between states and political parties and there is no good reason why it should not happen between religious and ideological groups. Does this then not involve some sort of syncretism? Certainly not, if the whole emphasis is on practical objectives rather than on basic philosophy. The Christian who believes that it is his duty to fight against racial discrimination, on the grounds of the Gospel, can work with the humanist, the Moslem, the Buddhist, yes, and also the communist who has the same objective but for other reasons. We can agree or disagree about our philosophies of life and yet engage together in practical tasks which we all want to see performed.

The World Council's CCIA has had conversations with communist politicians about disarmament. The Second Vatican Council's draft for Schema 13 says explicitly that believers and non-believers alike are called upon to work for human progress and that this cannot be done without a sincere dialogue although this must be prudent. No common doctrinal foundation is needed, no syncretistic compromise is involved, if men of different persuasions collaborate in an ad hoc fashion on specific common tasks in the field of social justice and international understanding. I underline that such collaboration in common tasks must be open to all and not take the form of a common front of some against others. It seems to me especially undesirable to create a common front of all the religious against the non-religious and anti-religious. For that presupposes that all the different religions have after all a common truth to defend and that is, once again, the common-denominator theory and the beginning of syncretism. Surely there are important objectives in the field of human progress for which we want to work and which are closer to the concerns of the secular world than to those of the traditional religious world.

What, then, is our conclusion? That we must not dream about what might be, but face the facts of life. We must get accustomed to the idea that, as far as we can see ahead today, no religious or philosophical or ideological creed is going to dominate the situation all alone and that we must therefore somehow learn the lesson what it means to coexist spiritually. None of our churches, none of us individually, is yet spiritually prepared for that situation. We have lived under the protection of our traditional cozy forms of Christendom. How will we behave when we have to navigate on the stormy seas of the open world society?

One thing is sure: the Christian church will once more be tested as by fire. It will have to show whether it is really built on the foundation once laid for all.

But is there any hope of reaching any form of world-community? Hardly in the sense of a worldwide spiritual-ideological consensus. But peaceful coexistence is possible without such a consensus if men become mature enough to respect each other as human beings, to develop a sense of solidarity, and to distinguish between the destructive warfare of violence and the spiritual battle for the souls and minds of men. That is a big "if," for we find on all sides the naïve idea that you can win a spiritual battle by the use of force. Our task is to fight that immature state of mind and to break through the obsession with physical armaments and to call men back to the really significant non-violent human battle for truth which is fought for all men, and does not destroy them.

Please do not think that the postscript which I now want to add is simply a commercial. Slightly modifying a slogan of the early days of the ecumenical movement, I would say: The pluralistic world-society is too tough for a divided church. That is not meant in the sense of "l'union fait la force" or a common front to defend whatever can be defended of our Christian positions. It is rather that a Christianity which spends so much of its time on internal conflicts has the wrong sense of proportion and is unable to play its role in the coming great conflict of religions and cultures. On the other hand, the realities of the pluralistic world will bring the churches closer together. Note the convergence of a number of basic positions between the Roman Catholic Church and the churches of the World Council. The pluralistic world throws us all back on the primary source of our faith and forces us to take a new look at the world around us. Thus pluralism can provide a real opportunity for a new united witness of the whole Church of Christ in and to the world.

Index of Names